Drafting
for the Creative Quilter

SALLY COLLINS

EASY TECHNIQUES FOR DESIGNING YOUR QUILTS, *YOUR WAY*

C&T PUBLISHING

Text copyright © 2010 by Sally Collins

Artwork copyright © 2010 by C&T Publishing, Inc.

Publisher: Amy Marson

Creative Director: Gailen Runge

Acquisitions Editor: Susanne Woods

Editor: Liz Aneloski

Technical Editors: Teresa Stroin and Joyce Lytle

Copyeditor/Proofreader: Wordfirm Inc.

Cover/Book Designer: Kerry Graham

Page Layout Artist: Casey Dukes

Production Coordinator: Zinnia Heinzmann

Production Editor: Julia Cianci

Illustrator: Lon Eric Craven

Photography by Christina Carty-Francis and Diane Pedersen of C&T Publishing, Inc., unless otherwise noted.

Published by C&T Publishing, Inc., P.O. Box 1456, Lafayette, CA 94549

Library of Congress Cataloging-in-Publication Data

Collins, Sally, 1946-

Drafting for the creative quilter : easy techniques for designing your quilts, your way / Sally Collins.

p. cm.

Includes bibliographical references.

ISBN 978-1-57120-802-6 (softcover)

1. Patchwork--Design. 2. Quilts--Design. I. Title.

TT835.C6473964 2010

746.46--dc22

2009046279

Printed in China

10 9 8 7 6 5 4 3

Dedication

To Sharyn Craig, a valued and admired friend. I thank you for sharing your expertise and information throughout your long career with such an open and generous heart. You made math clear and understandable and helped open the door to creative freedom for so many of us, your students; I aspire to do the same with this book. You continue to serve as a role model for me as a quiltmaker and teacher, and I am forever grateful for your generosity and kindness. You leave indelible footprints on my heart and the world of quiltmaking—thank you.

Acknowledgments

Writing books has always been exciting, fun, challenging, and at times frustrating, confusing, and overwhelming; and this book, my fifth, has been no different. Writing a book is not a solitary task; it takes many hearts, hands, and eyes to make an idea materialize. I thank each of you, from the bottom of my heart. Always, first, my husband, Joe, for continuing to support what I do and love me without question; my son, Sean, for all his patience, knowledge, information, and help on the Chrysanthemum block; Larry Axelrod, my friend Susan's husband, who is a wizard at math and answered any question I asked; my friend Glorianne Garza, who supports my work and gives honest, insightful help and critique; my friends Charlene Dakin, Marg Gair, and Nancy Elliott MacDonald, for kindly lending their beautiful quilts; Diana McClun and Laura Nownes, for sharing their Double Wedding Ring drafting instructions; Elaine Krajenke Ellison, who's eye-opening book, *Mathematical Quilts*, taught me so much. To all my students—I have learned so much from you. To C&T Publishing, for giving me the opportunity to share what I do again; to Liz Aneloski, developmental editor, who is absolutely the best; to my technical editors, Teresa Stroin and Joyce Lytle; to my book designer, Kerry Graham, and my illustrator, Lon Eric Craven; and to my production team, Zinnia Heinzmann and Julia Cianci.

I am forever grateful to you all.

Contents

Introduction

I became a quiltmaker in 1978, and from then throughout the early 1980s, I duplicated the quilts of others. It was all I knew, and I thoroughly loved that approach. I made quilts exactly as I saw them, including the exact fabrics. Following a pattern is a safe, sane, and largely successful way many quilters begin. If I had not done that, I wouldn't have been able to make quilts. Eventually, my own confidence grew with my skill development, and I began to make small changes in such things as color, fabric, or block orientation, but I had no idea how to change the size of blocks or designs.

Although my high-school education had not included subjects like algebra or geometry, I enrolled in a sampler quilt class that taught how to draft 12″ quilt blocks. I was thrilled, eager, and fearless. Sometimes ignorance is bliss. That class fueled my interest in the "mysterious" area of drafting and set loose my desire to make my own quilts, in my own way. That glimpse of complete creative freedom showed me the information I would need to acquire and develop my technical skills and my self-confidence in creating my own work. I will always be grateful for that wonderful, patient, quilt teacher from Moorpark, California, Charlotte Eckbach, because she helped open the door to creative freedom for me.

Since then, I have followed and admired the work of many great teachers and quiltmakers. The work of Jinny Beyer, Sharyn Craig, Marsha McCloskey, Judy Martin, and Joen Wolfrom has influenced me over the years. The quilts, books, and classes of these outstanding quiltmakers have been guiding lights along my own search for creative freedom. I learned to seek continuous improvement as I refined and advanced my drafting knowledge and workmanship. Learning to draft my own patterns has provided me with the opportunity to create unique quilts in any size I choose, with complete freedom and confidence in my ability to achieve a worthy manifestation of the thought in my mind.

As I travel and teach across the country, I frequently and regularly meet quiltmakers who are at the place I was when I signed up for that class with Charlotte Eckbach. These quilters are just as eager as I had been to be in charge of both the size and the composition of their quilts and to express their creative vision rather than duplicate the work of others. I think what holds them back most often is a simple lack of knowledge

and tools. This book is intended to serve that need; it can open that door to those quilters who have not yet acquired the knowledge and skill they need and seek for that freedom. For those who have already opened and explored that world of creativity, my design ideas, guidelines, and tools are here to make your journey a little easier.

With this book, I hope to share my drafting knowledge and approach to design with quilters and assist them in achieving the confidence and skill they need to bring their own ideas from thought to reality.

Included in these pages is a clear, detailed, concise accounting of how to draft blocks based on grids; how to draft blocks based on a circle; how to draft both simple and complex 8-pointed, 10-pointed, and Feathered Star blocks; how to design using mirrors, graph paper, pencil, and a calculator; how to fracture the basic structure of traditional blocks to create your own unique designs; and more, all in the size you choose.

The three projects in this book are presented in their order of challenge. To ensure success, I suggest you read through the instructions carefully before beginning each project. Feel free to make size or design changes to any of them. Refer to either Designing on an Overall Grid (page 71) or Designing within Traditional Blocks (page 79). Adding or eliminating elements changes the design and makes it uniquely your own. You will obviously need your usual sewing supplies. Total fabric requirements for each project are provided. Creativity begins with one small step; there is no risk. Explore, have fun, and enjoy.

I invite you to turn the page and join me on this journey toward creative freedom.

Drafting

Welcome to Drafting

Although this book will introduce and explain a variety of drafting categories (grid based, circular, log cabin/pineapple, and 8-pointed star), it is important to understand that each category has its own process, or series of steps, necessary to complete its drafting. This process is cumulative rather than singular, meaning that no one step is more or less important than any other step. They are all equal, and each must be done precisely and in concert with the others. Any inaccuracies, however small, will negatively affect the design. Inaccuracies will lead to shapes not fitting exactly, block size changing, blocks not square, and so forth. You will find yourself continually compensating for any drafting errors throughout the sewing process. Thus, remaining focused and aware at each step is critical to success. The quality of your work is a reflection of how well you execute the process.

◆◆◆◆◆◆ Noteworthy ◆◆◆◆◆◆

Whenever you draft, design, calculate, or figure out anything in patchwork, you are never including seam allowance. Seam allowance is only relevant when you begin to cut and sew your fabric.

When drafting, you will create your design in actual size, so you can see exactly what size each individual shape will be. This will help you choose designs compatible with your piecing skills—in general, the more pieces in a block, the more sewing skill is required. If you are new to drafting, it will be beneficial to read, draft, and follow the book sequentially and experience all the categories, in order, to gain confidence and drafting skill.

The information and skill development offered in each chapter are cumulative and sometimes relate to the next or previous chapters.

The ability to draft your own blocks or designs in the size you choose will advance your creative skills. It will also be fun, exciting, sometimes challenging, and always satisfying. Drafting gives you the opportunity and option to change your design by adding lines, eliminating lines, changing lines, or sometimes drawing a line "incorrectly," which is often how original designs are created.

Pattern drafting begins with and relies on the ability to recognize and understand the underlying architecture of patchwork. Once you can distinguish between a grid-based category and an 8-pointed star category, from a hexagon category and a circular category, you have unlocked the door to creative freedom.

◆◆◆◆◆◆ Noteworthy ◆◆◆◆◆◆

I always use either 8- or 10-to-the-inch cross-sectioned graph paper when I draft. This paper makes it easier to draw an accurate square. I can also use the graph paper lines as guidelines to draw accurate horizontal, vertical, and 45° lines.

Important Information on Accuracy

Drafting lines are not drawn randomly or arbitrarily. Rather, they are drawn exactly and precisely. Based on your individual design, you will often be connecting corners, midpoints, or corners to midpoints. Take extreme care at each step.

- Use a mechanical pencil for a consistently thin line.

- Use a light touch—only you need to see your lines, and light lines will be much easier to erase.

- Position your light source on the side of the ruler where your pencil is to avoid shadows.

- Use either 8- or 10-to-the-inch cross-sectioned graph paper (darkened blue lines at 1-inch increments).

- To prevent smudging and to enable yourself to see your previously drawn line(s), work from right to left when drawing vertical lines for grids (do the opposite if you are left handed). When drawing lines horizontally, work from top to bottom rather than from bottom to top for the same reason.

- To accurately draw a line that travels exactly from one point to another, place the ruler's edge just next to, not on, the beginning and ending points to accommodate the width of the pencil lead. The pencil line is what must travel exactly from point to point.

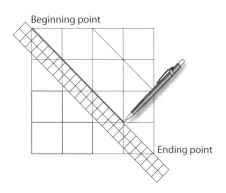

Beginning point

Ending point

◆◆◆◆◆◆ **Noteworthy** ◆◆◆◆◆◆

One way to make sure that your line travels accurately from point to point is to use the lead of the pencil to align the ruler edge. Place the pencil point exactly where you want the line to begin, then slide the ruler edge next to the pencil and align the rest of the ruler edge where the line will end. While holding the ruler in place, move the pencil to the end point and make any needed ruler adjustments to be sure the ruler edge is snug against the pencil lead. Move the pencil back to the beginning point and draw the line.

- When drawing diagonal 45° lines on graph paper (corner to corner on a square), the drawn line must travel exactly from corner to corner on all the small squares on the graph paper.

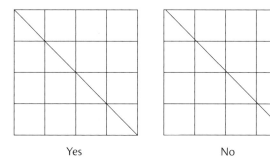

Yes   No

Seven Simple Steps to Drafting Your Way to Creative Freedom

Refer to pages 14–16 for more detail.

1. Choose a pattern or block design.

2. Determine its drafting category and underlying grid formation.

3. Decide the size of the block you want to make.

4. Determine the size of the grid needed to make the block the size you want.

5. Draw a square the chosen block size; then add, connect, and erase lines to draw your block.

6. Identify the different shapes needed to sew the block and determine the logical sewing sequence.

7. Add seam allowances to each shape, cut fabric, and assemble the block.

It's as easy as that!

Tools and Supplies

The tools you use to draft are important to the success of the process and will reflect the work you do.

1. Accurate cross-section graph paper in 4-, 8-, and 10-to-the-inch increments—I use both 8½″ × 11″ and 17″ × 22″ tablets. If your designs are larger, you can tape sheets of graph paper together.

2. Compass that holds its position

3. Yardstick compass for designs larger than the span of your compass (page 20)

4. Mechanical pencil

5. Good eraser, such as a white art eraser or gum eraser

6. Rulers: 1″ × 6″, 2″ × 12″, and/or 2″ × 18″ red-lined see-through rulers—I recommend the rulers from The C-Thru Ruler Company. These rulers are preferred over rotary cutting rulers for drafting because they are thin and lay flat to the paper.

7. Protractor: half-circle and full-circle—The full-circle protractor makes it much easier to draft circles.

8. Colored pencils (optional): 6 different colors (red, blue, orange, green, yellow, and aqua) to clarify and distinguish different drafting lines

9. Handheld calculator

10. Mirrors for designing (page 91)

Drafting tools and supplies

Grid-Based Blocks

GRID FORMATION

Grid formation simply means that the size of the square on which you will develop your design is divided into an equal number of grids across and down. Many patchwork blocks and designs are developed on a grid of equal-sized squares across and down, much like a checkerboard. The first thing you need to learn on your journey to creative freedom is how to determine which grid you should base a particular block on. This is important because you draw the grid first, and then you use the grid to add additional lines to draw the block.

The four grid-based families in patchwork are 4-patch, 9-patch, 5-patch, and 7-patch.

Four-Patch Drafting Category

For example, a block in the 4-patch family can be divided into 4 equal divisions (2 × 2 grid formation). If you divide each grid in half vertically and horizontally, you have 16 equal divisions (4 × 4 grid formation); or if you divide the grids in half again, you have 64 equal divisions (8 × 8 grid formation); and so on. Each grid formation is in the 4-patch family because the total number of equal divisions is divisible by 4, and the divisions are multiples of 4 (4, 16, 64).

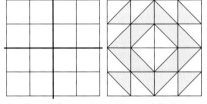

4 × 4 grid formation; 16 equal divisions

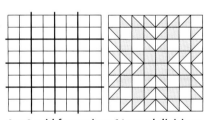

8 × 8 grid formation; 64 equal divisions

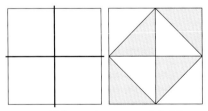

2 × 2 grid formation; 4 equal divisions

Nine-Patch Drafting Category

The math is the same for the 9-patch family. The square can have 9 equal divisions (3 × 3 grid formation); 36 equal divisions (6 × 6 grid formation); or, if divided in half again, 144 equal divisions (12 × 12 grid formation). The total number of equal divisions (9, 36, 144) is divisible by 9, and the divisions are multiples of 9.

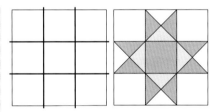

3 × 3 grid formation; 9 equal divisions

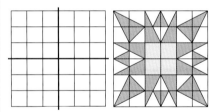

6 × 6 grid formation; 36 equal divisions

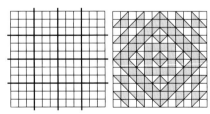

12 × 12 grid formation; 144 equal divisions

DRAFTING FOR THE CREATIVE QUILTER

Five-Patch Drafting Category

The 5-patch family is different in that the square is divided into a 5 × 5 grid formation, or 25 equal divisions, not into 5 pieces. The square can, however, be divided as explained with 4-patch and 9-patch, for example, into 100 equal divisions (10 × 10 grid formation). The total number of equal divisions is divisible by 5, and the divisions are multiples of 5.

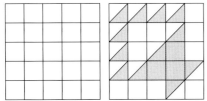

5 × 5 grid formation; 25 equal divisions

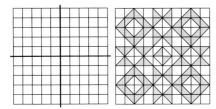

10 × 10 grid formation; 100 equal divisions

Seven-Patch Drafting Category

The 7-patch family is similar to the 5-patch in that the square is not divided into 7 pieces but rather into a 7 × 7 grid formation with 49 equal divisions, or into a 14 × 14 grid formation with 196 equal divisions. The total number of equal divisions is divisible by 7, and the divisions are multiples of 7.

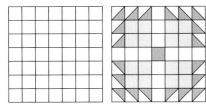

7 × 7 grid formation; 49 equal divisions

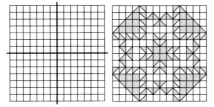

14 × 14 grid formation; 196 equal divisions

How to Determine the Underlying Grid Formation

Remember that a grid formation is based on equal-sized squares. To help recognize and determine into which grid formation a block falls, try one or more of the following options.

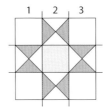

Option 1: Count the number of equal divisions across the top or side edge of a block.

Option 2: Count the number of equal divisions along an edge-to-edge seam.

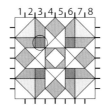

Option 3: Identify the smallest piece and count.

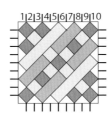

Option 4: Follow equidistant intersections, although they may not be in the same row.

Once the square has been drawn and divided into the appropriate grid formation (5 × 5, 6 × 6, 8 × 8, 7 × 7, etc.), the design is drafted by referencing your photo or sketch as you connect corners and mid-points, drawing lines to previous intersections or erasing lines over the grid. This creates shapes such as rectangles, triangles, parallelograms, trapezoids, and diamonds that are superimposed over the grid. Nothing is random or arbitrary. Erase all unneeded lines so that the remaining lines are seamlines. Shapes can occupy the space of only one grid or of multiple grids. Larger shapes are often the size of multiples of the smallest shape.

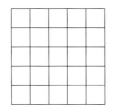

Square with grid formation

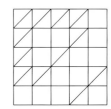

Design superimposed over grid

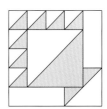

Seamlines remain.

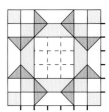

Center square occupies (and is the size of) three grids.

Play the
GRID GAME

See if you can recognize the underlying grid formation needed to draft these 20 blocks (answers follow).

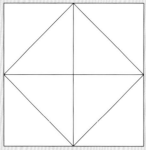

A. Broken Dishes

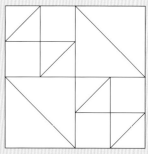

E. Crosses and Losses

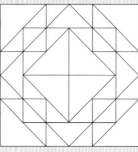

B. Mother's Favorite

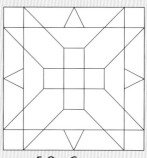

F. Our Country

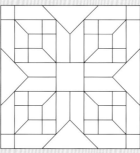

C. Granny's Favorite

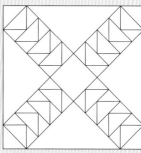

G. Wild Goose Chase

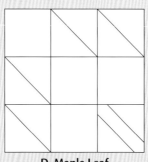

D. Maple Leaf

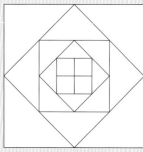

H. Snail's Trail

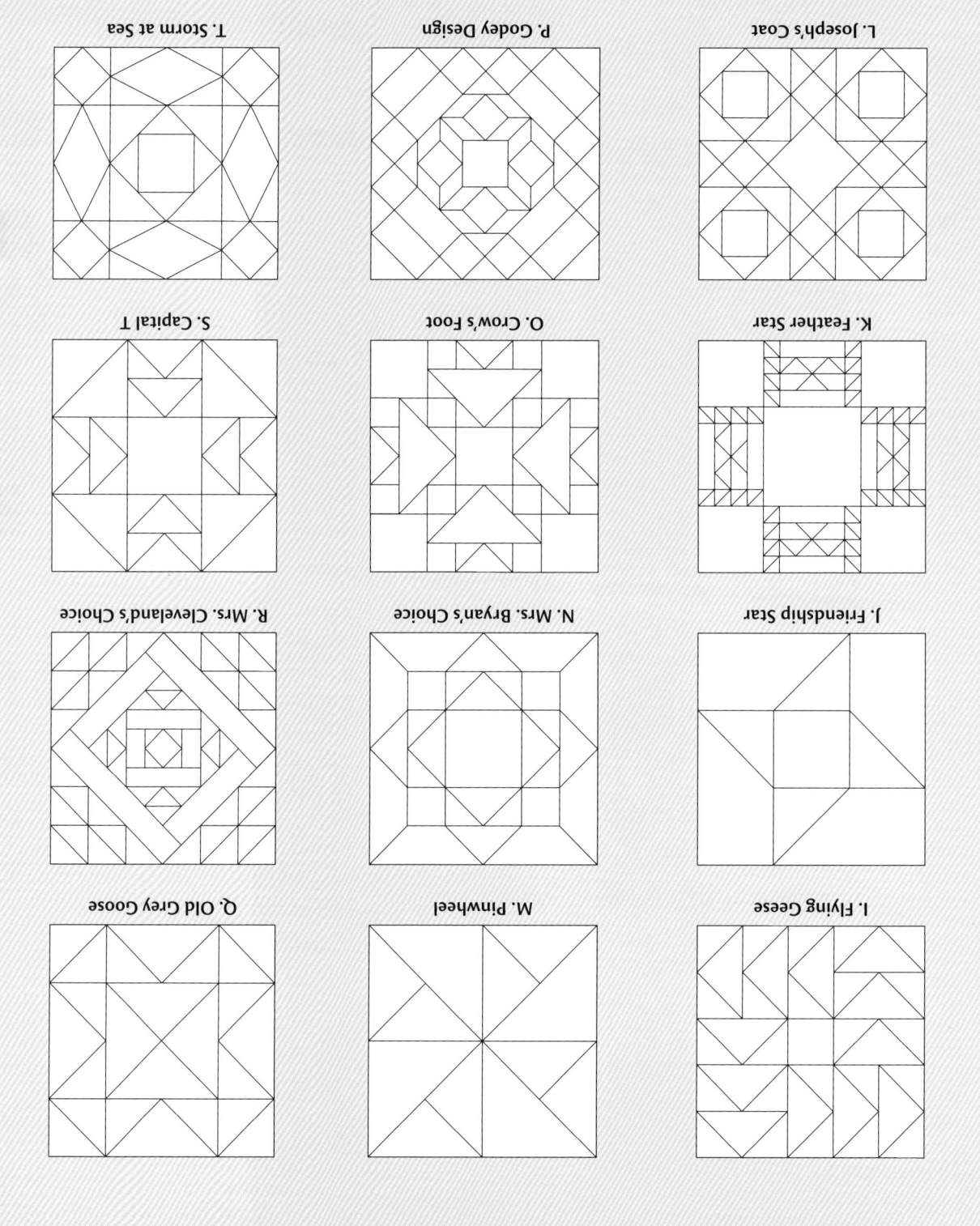

T. Storm at Sea   P. Godey Design   L. Joseph's Coat
S. Capital T   O. Crow's Foot   K. Feather Star
R. Mrs. Cleveland's Choice   N. Mrs. Bryan's Choice   J. Friendship Star
Q. Old Grey Goose   M. Pinwheel   I. Flying Geese

LET'S START DRAFTING

Once you are able to recognize the underlying grid formation of patchwork blocks, its time to test the waters. I invite you to assemble your graph paper, rulers, pencil, and eraser and join me as I go through the sequential steps of drafting a grid-based block. Reading the text and looking at the illustrations and photos, although important, will not give you necessary hands-on experience. Doing is the key to learning, knowing, and understanding.

♦♦♦ Noteworthy ♦♦♦

Whenever you draft, design, calculate, or figure out anything in patchwork, you never include seam allowance until you're ready for fabric.

Please read through this entire section before you start. You will not actually use paper, pencil, and ruler until Step 6.

1. Get out all tools, rulers, and graph paper (page 9).

2. Choose a pattern or block design. We will draft a Sawtooth Star.

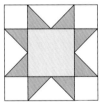

Sawtooth Star

3. Determine its drafting category and underlying grid formation.

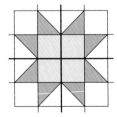

Sawtooth Star, 4-patch drafting category, 4 × 4 grid formation, 16 equal divisions

4. Decide the size of the block. Although quilt blocks can be drafted in any size you desire (page 17), it is easiest to choose a size that is equally divisible by the basic grid. For example, the Sawtooth Star is drafted on a 4 × 4 grid, so it is easily drafted in any size square that is obviously equally divisible by 4 (4", 6", 8", 12"). We will draft a 6" Sawtooth Star.

♦♦♦ Noteworthy ♦♦♦

Don't forget about less obvious block sizes. For example a 5" block ÷ 4 = 1¼" grid. A 5½" block ÷ 4 = 1.375, or 1⅜", grid (see Decimal Equivalent Chart, page 68).

5. Determine the grid dimension (the size of each individual grid) by dividing the block size by its number of equal divisions. For our example, 6" block ÷ 4 equal divisions = 1½" grid dimension. I use a small hand-held calculator for all my "figuring out." If your answer is not a whole number, translate three decimal places into fractions (see Decimal Equivalent Chart, page 68) or tenths to determine which graph paper to use (10-to-the-inch or 8-to-the-inch). Knowing the grid dimension not only gives you the information you need to draw the grid but also allows you to measure your patchwork as you sew (page 16).

6. Draw the chosen size of square (6") on 8-to-the-inch graph paper and lightly draw the grid formation within the square. Here's where, together, we put pencil to paper and walk through the door to creative freedom!

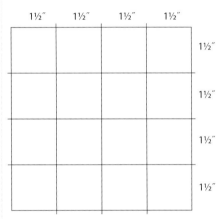

6" square divided into a 4 × 4 grid at 1½" intervals

♦♦♦ Noteworthy ♦♦♦

You could easily change the size of your block by changing (or choosing) the grid dimension. For example, if your grid dimension is 2", you would multiply 2" (grid dimension) by the number of equal divisions (4), which yields an 8" block. If the grid is 1¼", you would have a 5" block; if the grid dimension is 3", you would have a 12" block. Multiplying the grid dimension by the number of equal divisions determines the size of the block.

7. Develop the block design by connecting and erasing lines to subdivide the grid into shapes such as rectangles, trapezoids, parallelograms, diamonds, and so forth. Refer to your photo or sketch for guidance until the design is complete. Begin with the largest shapes; the smaller ones will develop and become apparent. When you are finished drafting the block, erase all lines that are not seams (not all grid lines are seamlines). You should have only seamlines remaining.

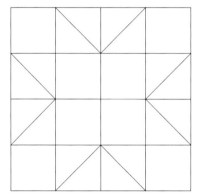

Subdivide the grid into
the Sawtooth Star.

8. Identify the different shapes needed to sew the block and add their grainlines. Keep the straight of grain on the outside edges of the block. In the Sawtooth Star, there are 4 shapes: 2 right-angle triangles (1 large and 1 smaller) and 2 squares (1 large and 1 smaller). These are shapes A, B, C, and D. For stability, it's important that the straight of grain be placed on the outside edge of blocks. However, I never sacrifice design for straight grain. If there is a particular area of a fabric I want to place within a shape and it results in bias at the edge of the block or shape, I just sew and press carefully.

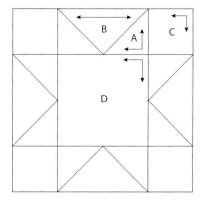

Identify the shapes and place grainlines.

9. Examine the design and determine the logical sewing sequence to piece and press the block. One way to do this is to first find the longest lines that identify a row (usually, but not always, they will run from edge to edge horizontally, vertically, or diagonally). Blocks are usually assembled by first joining pieces into units, then units into rows, then rows into the completed block.

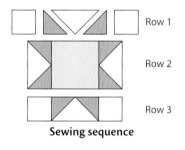

Row 1

Row 2

Row 3

Sewing sequence

10. Isolate each individual shape, add a ¼″ seam allowance on all sides, and use your favorite cutting and sewing techniques for assembly. This step allows you to sew the design properly. When measuring a shape for cutting, if the dimensions are easily found on the ruler, then rotary cutting is the method preferred by most quilters. However, if the cutting dimensions are not easily found on the ruler, or if you want to custom cut a shape from a particular area of a fabric, make a template for that shape (page 90).

How to Determine Grid Dimension

Many square patchwork blocks are developed on a grid of equal divisions across and down a square. *Grid dimension*, which refers to the finished size of each individual grid square, determines the size of the block. Knowing the block's grid dimension will also allow you to measure your patchwork as you sew.

To measure your work as you sew, you must first know the grid dimension. You can determine this information in one of two ways.

- Choose the block pattern you want to sew (e.g., Sawtooth Star), identify the underlying grid formation (4 × 4), and choose a block size (6″). To determine the grid dimension, simply **divide** the size of the block by the number of equal divisions across the block. For example, 6″ (block size) ÷ 4 (number of equal divisions across the block) = 1½″ grid dimension.

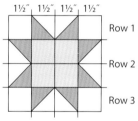

1½″ 1½″ 1½″ 1½″

Row 1

Row 2

Row 3

6″ Sawtooth Star block

- Another way to determine the grid dimension of a block is to choose it. For example, let's say you want to make a Sawtooth Star block (4 patch, 4 × 4 grid formation), and you are comfortable sewing in a 1″ finished grid. The block size is determined by **multiplying** the grid dimension (1″) by the number of equal divisions across the block (4), so 1″ × 4 = 4″ block size. I sometimes choose the grid dimension if I'm making only one block or if I'm doing a repeat-block quilt, because then the size of the block is not as important as working in a grid dimension that I'm comfortable with.

If the grid dimension plus seam allowance is not ruler-friendly (the smallest fraction I use with rulers is ¹/₁₆) and I'm using templates for cutting, I use the template to evaluate and monitor the patchwork. Refer to Templates (page 90).

Using Grid Dimension to Measure Patchwork

Let's assume that we're going to sew the 6″ Sawtooth Star block that has a grid dimension of 1½″ (remember, the grid dimension does not include seam allowances). The fabric is cut (including seam allowances), the pieces and units are created, the block is laid out, and we are ready to sew together the first two pieces of Row 1.

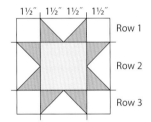

TO MEASURE YOUR WORK, FOLLOW THESE STEPS:

1. Add the number of grids you have sewn together (in this case, 3).

◆◆◆◆◆◆ Noteworthy ◆◆◆◆◆◆

When measuring, whenever a shape or unit takes up the space of more than one grid, it gets credit for the number of grids it occupies.

2. Multiply the number of grids sewn (3) by the grid dimension (1½″).

3. Add ½″ for seam allowance, always. This means that for the Sawtooth Star block, 3 grids × 1½″ = 4½″ + ½″ for seam allowances = 5″. The first 3 grids of Row 1 should measure 5″ from edge to edge. If they do, great; if they do not, either the cutting or the sewing is in question. Do not continue adding grids until the first 3 measure 5″. When these 3 grids measure 5″, forget this number and continue.

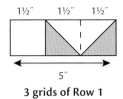

3 grids of Row 1

4. Add the next piece of Row 1 to those already sewn. Because you have now added another grid, you must repeat Steps 1–3 to measure your work from edge to edge. The piece should now measure 6½″ (4 grids × 1½″ grid dimension = 6″ + ½″ for seam allowances = 6½″).

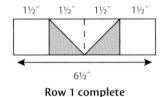

Row 1 complete

Now you can draw and sew any grid-based block in any size you need!

DRAFTING FOR THE CREATIVE QUILTER

HOW TO DRAFT ANY SIZE SQUARE INTO ANY SIZE GRID

Sometimes the size of the block you want or need will not be easily divisible by the grid of the block design. For example, to draft a 6″ Bear's Paw block, which is a 7 × 7 grid formation, you need to divide a 6″ square by 7. On a calculator, 6 ÷ 7 = 0.857, which is not a ruler-friendly number and which, unless you have 7-to-the-inch graph paper, is challenging to draft accurately. The following, long-standing technique drafts any size square into any size grid. The size of your square does not need to be a whole number (12″, 8″, etc.); it can be any size you wish (11⅜″, 7⅝″, 9³⁄₁₆″, etc.).

♦♦♦♦♦♦ Noteworthy ♦♦♦♦♦♦

You can use plain or graph paper for this technique; however, I always use 8-to-the-inch graph paper. Although the drawn grid lines will not usually be on the blue graph paper lines, I use the graph paper lines in concert with the horizontal and vertical red lines of the C-Thru ruler to ensure that the grid lines I draw are exactly straight (the red line grid of the ruler is also in eighths). This drafting technique is simple in theory, but great care must be taken to ensure that all drawn grid lines are straight, accurate, and at a perfect right angle to the square's top and bottom lines. If they are not straight, the individual squares within the grid will not all be the same size or shape. Step 5 explains in detail how I use the C-Thru ruler and graph paper together.

1. Draw the size square you desire (in this case, 6″ × 6″) on 8-to-the-inch graph paper. Label the 4 corners 1, 2, 3, and 4.

2. Find a measurement on your ruler that is larger than the block size and divisible by 7 (the number of equal divisions across and down). That would be the 7″ mark on your ruler. Seven is divisible by 7 and is larger than the 6″ block you chose (7″ ÷ 7 = 1″).

3. Position the corner of your ruler on the left bottom corner (#1) of your 6″ × 6″ square. Angle the ruler up until the 7″ mark on the ruler is exactly on the right side line of the 6″ square.

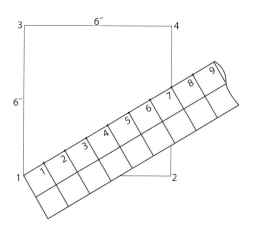

♦♦♦♦♦♦ Noteworthy ♦♦♦♦♦♦

■ Another option is to place the 1″ mark of the ruler in the corner and add 1″ to the number placed on the right side line of the square (8″). If you employ this option, do not forget to add the 1″ to the number on the right side.

■ If the number you need does not fit on the square, just extend the right edge line up to allow the ruler to reach the desired number. For example a 9″ block ÷ 7 = 1.2857. The next whole number evenly divisible by 7 is 14. 14 ÷ 7 = 2. Mark every 2″, and then draw vertical grid lines. When you rotate the paper to get the horizontal lines, extend the right edge line again.

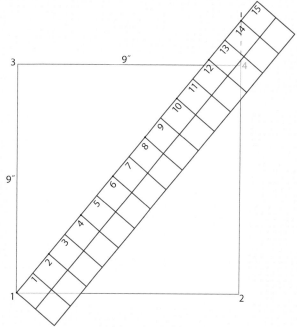

Extending right edge line

4. Mark a dot on your paper every 1″ (this is the number you arrived at by dividing 7 into 7 in Step 3). Mark dots exactly, not casually, angling your pencil lead inward, close to the ruler's edge.

5. Draw the first set of grid lines using the dots, blue graph paper lines, and the C-Thru ruler's red lines as follows:

a. Starting at the first dot on the right side of the square (or on the left side if you are left handed), position the ruler edge next to the dot, allowing for the width of the pencil lead. The line you will draw must travel through the center of the dot.

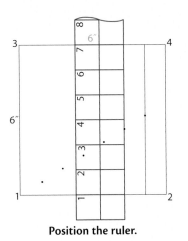

Position the ruler.

b. Now move the ruler slightly up or down and align a horizontal red line of the ruler over both the top and bottom lines of the square. If your square size is in 1/16 of an inch, to ensure that you're drawing an exact straight line, be sure the red lines of the ruler are equidistant from and parallel to the blue lines of the graph paper.

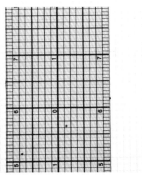

Close-up of red ruler lines and graph paper blue lines

c. Holding the ruler in place and focusing on one blue line, look through the ruler and check that the blue vertical lines of the graph paper and the red lines of the ruler are equidistant from each other from the top of the square to the bottom. If they are not, adjust the ruler so they are and then draw the line. Repeat this process for each dot.

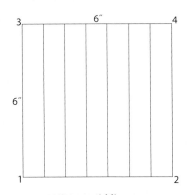

Draw grid lines.

6. Turn your paper a quarter turn and repeat Steps 3–5 to complete the 7 × 7 grid in the 6″ × 6″ square. This grid will allow you to draft the Bear's Paw block or any 7-patch block that is 6″ × 6″.

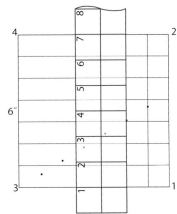

Dividing a 6″ × 6″ square into a 7 × 7 grid

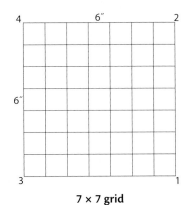

7 × 7 grid

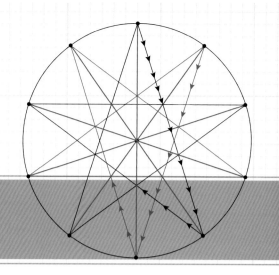

Circular Designs

In addition to the usual tools of graph paper, pencil, ruler, and eraser, circular designs require a compass (a tool used to draw partial or full circles, determine midpoints, and hold measurements), a protractor (a tool used to determine angles), a rotary cutting mat, and removable tape.

Circle: A closed plane curve such that all its points are equidistant from the center

Diameter: The measurement across the circle, through the center from one side to the opposite side (the size of the circle)

Radius: The measurement from the center of the circle to its edge (half the diameter)

Circumference: The distance around the edge of the circle

Arc: Any part of a curved line

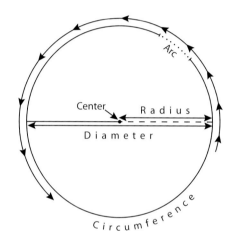

HOW TO USE A COMPASS TO DRAW A CIRCLE

The most important feature of a compass is its ability to hold its set position firmly. One with a crossbar and a wheel is most dependable, though for years I have used an inexpensive school compass and a disposable mechanical pencil. I like the mechanical pencil, because it provides a consistent line weight without having to sharpen it. To prevent the pivot point from slipping or moving, and to keep the graph paper in place, position a rotary cutting mat under your graph paper and tape your graph paper to the mat. Pushing the pivot point of the compass through the paper into the mat will help keep the pivot point in place while drawing.

1. Choose the size of the circle (e.g., 6″).

2. To draw a circle with a compass, open the compass the distance of the radius (e.g., a 6″ circle has a 3″ radius).

✦✦✦✦✦✦ **Noteworthy** ✦✦✦✦✦✦

A standard compass opens to approximately 6″, which allows you to draw a circle approximately 12″. One way to draw larger circles is to use a yardstick compass, which can be found at any art supply or drafting store, as well as at some quilt shops. The yardstick compass has two separate pieces (one is the pivot point and one is the pencil) that each attach to a yardstick or long ruler.

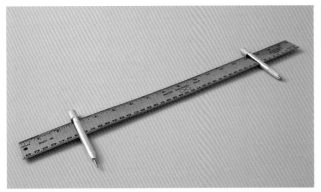

Yardstick compass on ruler for drawing large circles

3. Push the pivot point of the compass through the paper and into the mat. (This will be the center of the circle.) Expand the compass until the pencil and pivot point are 3″ apart on the graph paper. If you are using plain paper, use a ruler as a guide when expanding the compass.

4. Holding the top of the compass perpendicular to the paper, draw one half of the circle.

5. Leaving the pivot point in place, return the pencil to the beginning point and draw the remaining half. The line of any circle should be exactly continuous.

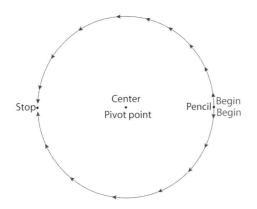

Draw half the circle (shown in blue), then draw the other half (shown in red).

DRUNKARD'S PATH BLOCK

This simple block is created by drawing an arc, rather than a complete circle, giving you a chance to practice using the compass. This block is commonly divided into the proportion, or ratio, of ⅓ square to ⅔ arc. But you can choose any proportion you like.

Drunkard's Path block

TO DRAFT A 6″ (FINISHED) BLOCK:

1. Draw a 6″ square on graph paper.

2. To determine where to draw the arc, which is ⅔ of the square, divide 6″ by 3, which equals 2″ (⅓), then double it to equal 4″ (⅔).

3. Make a mark 4″ from one corner on 2 sides of the square. Place the pivot point of the compass at the same corner. Expand the pencil point to exactly reach the 4″ mark. Leaving the pivot point in place, draw the arc from one 4″ mark to the other.

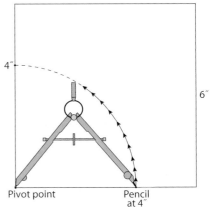

Draw a square; then draw the arc.

DRAFTING FOR THE CREATIVE QUILTER

GRANDMOTHER'S FAN BLOCK

The basic Fan block is often referred to as the Grandmother's Fan. It is drafted within a quarter of a circle (so, four fans create a complete circle). Depending on the complexity of the fan, this block has the potential to create a variety of designs, such as Dresden Plate, Mariner's Compass, Sunflower, Sunburst, and other symmetrical circular designs. Learning to draft this block enables you to make all the choices regarding size, number of segments, and segment design.

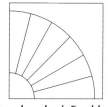

Grandmother's Fan block

A traditional Grandmother's Fan block consists of a background area, a handle, and segments. Arcs (partial circles) can be drawn any size and from any corner within the square. When designing the blocks, be sure to keep a pleasing visual proportion between the areas and consider your sewing skill. The segments have a smooth edge, and the number of segments within this area is up to you. However, because you will be working within a corner of a square that is 90°, it is usually easiest to choose a number of segments that will divide evenly into 90°. Decide how many segments you want, then divide that number into 90° to find the angle of the segments.

TO DRAFT A 6″ (FINISHED) BLOCK:

1. Draw a 6″ square on graph paper.

2. For the handle arc, make a mark 1⅝″ from the corner. For the outer edge of the fan arc, make a mark 5½″ from the same corner. Place the pivot point of the compass at that same corner and expand the compass pencil to reach the 1⅝″ mark. Draw an arc from one side to the opposite side. Repeat for the 5½″ mark.

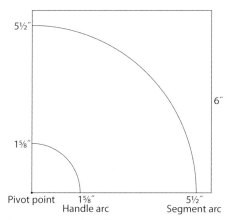

Draw a square, handle arc, and segment arc.

3. Position the protractor over the square, so that the crosshair is over the same corner. The protractor's 90° mark is on the vertical line extending from that corner, and the 0° mark is on the horizontal line extending from the same corner.

4. Decide how many segments you want for the fan. For now, let's choose six: 90° ÷ 6 segments = 15°. Determine all the degree markings and write them down before starting to mark the block. You are simply adding multiples of the degree angle for each segment—in our case,

this is 15°, so you would mark at 15, 30, 45, 60, and 75. Hold the protractor in place. For six segments, mark dots close to the edge of the protractor at exactly 15°, 30°, 45°, 60°, and 75°.

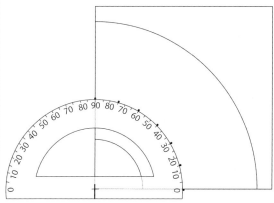

Determine and mark degrees for 6 segments.

✦✦✦✦✦✦ Noteworthy ✦✦✦✦✦✦

The dots that you mark on your paper using the protractor can be anywhere in relationship to the square. What is important is the corner where the crosshair marking on the protractor is positioned. You will always align the ruler's edge with the corner where the crosshair marking was positioned and each degree dot.

5. Remove the protractor. Align the edge of a ruler so it lies along the corner where the crosshair marking was positioned and along the 15° dot. Be sure your ruler edge is just next to, not on, the corner and dot to accommodate the width of the pencil lead. Draw the line between the handle and segment arcs only. Repeat for the remaining degree markings to complete the fan. All 6 segments should be exactly the same width.

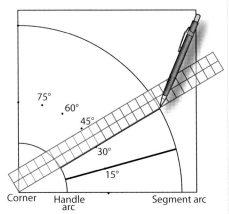

Draw segment lines.

Now that you have some experience using a compass and protractor, try these design variations, which are simple to accomplish and can be added to the basic fan we just drafted. Once you understand the process, you will be creating your own designs in no time. On any of the styles covered here, if you place your mirrors (page 91) along the dashed lines, you will see the complete circular design, which potentially creates a Dresden Plate, Mariner's Compass, Sunflower, Sunburst, and so forth. To make design changes to the basic fan, you will need to do two things: add reference arcs and determine the midpoint of the curved lines or segments. For these, you will need the compass and protractor.

SCALLOPED-EDGE FAN BLOCK

This block adds a curve to the smooth edge of the fan. When multiplied by four, it creates a lovely Dresden Plate block.

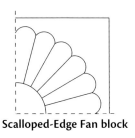

Scalloped-Edge Fan block

TO DRAFT A 6″ (FINISHED) BLOCK:

1. Draw a 6″ square on graph paper.

2. Draw a handle arc 1⅝″ from the corner, a reference arc 4¾″ from the corner, and a segment arc 5″ from the corner. (See Step 2 on page 21 for more details.) The scallop will be added above the segment arc line.

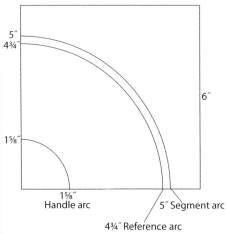

Draw a handle, reference, and segment arcs.

3. Using your protractor, divide the fan into 6 segments: 15°, 30°, 45°, 60°, and 75°. (See Steps 3–5 on pages 21–22 for more details.)

The distance between the reference arc and the segment arc determines the height of the scallop. The further the reference arc is from the segment arc, the flatter the scallop will be; the closer it is to the segment arc, the higher the scallop will be.

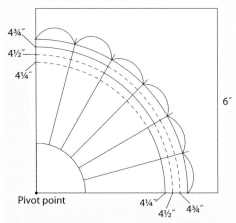

3 different reference arcs (4¼″, 4½″, 4¾″) and the resulting scallops

4. To find and mark the midpoint of each segment for the scallop placement (half of 15° is 7.5°), position the protractor. Beginning at one edge of the square, make a mark at 7.5° on the reference arc. From there, make 5 marks at 15° increments: 22.5°, 37.5°, 52.5°, 67.5°, and 82.5°.

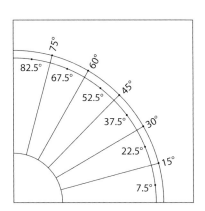

Find and mark the midpoint of each segment.

Another way to divide any curved or straight line in half is to place the pivot point of the compass at one end of the line you wish to divide in half. Expand the compass so the pencil point is beyond the halfway mark—do this by eye. Move the pencil upward to make an arc. Leaving the expanded compass in the same position, place the pivot point at the opposite end of the line and repeat. Where the arcs intersect is the midpoint of the line. Align your ruler edge with the handle corner and the arc intersection, and then mark the midpoint of each segment.

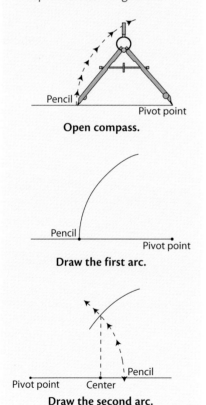

Open compass.

Draw the first arc.

Draw the second arc.

5. To draw the scallop, place the pivot point of the compass at the midpoint of a segment on the reference arc. Place the pencil point on one side of that segment and rotate the compass pencil to the other side of the segment. Repeat for each segment.

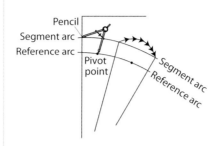

Draw a scallop.

SUNFLOWER BLOCK

The curves or petals on this design are longer than those on a scalloped edge and end in a point.

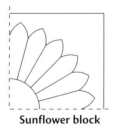

Sunflower block

TO DRAFT A 6˝ (FINISHED) BLOCK:

1. Draw a 6˝ square.

2. Draw the handle (1⅝˝) and the segment arc (4½˝), which, in this case, indicates the lowest point between 2 petals. The petals will be on top of the segment arc. (See Step 2 on page 21 for more details.) Because this design has a longer, pointed scalloped edge and thus requires more space than the more traditional scallop (page 22), the segment arc will be lower. There is no reference arc for this design.

3. Using the protractor, divide the fan into 6 segments: 15°, 30°, 45°, 60°, 75°. (See Steps 3–5 on pages 21–22 for more details.)

4. Place the pivot point of the compass on one side of a segment and the pencil end at the opposite side of a segment. Swivel the pencil upward, creating an arc. Repeat from the opposite side of the segment. The petal design extends to where the 2 arcs intersect.

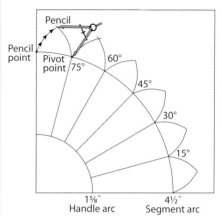

Draw a handle arc, segment arc, 6 segments, and petals.

DIRECTIONAL POINTED-EDGE FAN BLOCK

Pointed-Edge Fan blocks can be directional or symmetrical. Directional Pointed-Edge Fan blocks look more like a traditional fan style, as if the fan is closed and then quickly slides open. This fan block employs a reference arc in addition to the usual handle and segment arcs. The reference arc is drawn between the other two arcs because the design is developed within the perimeter of the segment arc.

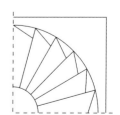

Directional Pointed-Edge Fan block

TO DRAFT A 6″ (FINISHED) BLOCK:

1. Draw a 6″ square on graph paper.

2. Using the compass, draw a handle arc (1⅝″) and a segment arc (5½″), which, in this case, indicates the maximum amount of design space and the boundary of the segments. (See Step 2 on page 21 for more details.) Because the design of this fan will be developed inside the segment arc, draw a reference arc (4⅞″) between the 2 arcs.

3. Using the protractor, divide the square into 6 segments: 15°, 30°, 45°, 60°, 75°. (See Steps 3–5 on pages 21–22 for more details.)

4. Draw a line from the segment arc diagonally to the reference arc. Repeat for the remaining 5 segments.

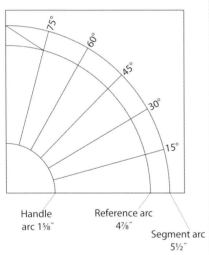

Draw handle, segment, and reference arcs; then divide the square into 6 segments and develop the point.

♦♦♦ Noteworthy ♦♦♦

The distance between the reference arc and the segment arc determines the segment's angle. The greater the distance between the reference arc and the segment arc, the sharper the angle. Try different distances between these two arcs to see what designs emerge.

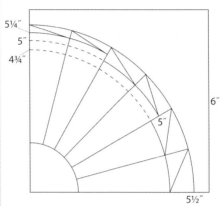

Three different reference arc placements: 4¾″, 5″, and 5¼″

SYMMETRICAL POINTED-EDGE FAN BLOCK

As stated earlier, Pointed-Edge Fan blocks can be directional or symmetrical. To give the symmetrical Pointed-Edge Fan blocks a three-dimensional appearance, split each segment in half lengthwise between a light and dark value. This block employs a reference arc in addition to the usual handle arc and segment arc. The reference arc is drawn between the two arcs because the design is developed within the perimeter of the segment arc.

Symmetrical Pointed-Edge Fan block

TO DRAFT A 6″ (FINISHED) BLOCK:

1. Draw a 6″ square on graph paper.

2. Using the compass, draw the handle arc (1⅝″) and segment arc (5½″), which, in this case, indicates the maximum design area and serves as a boundary for the segments. (See Step 2 on page 21 for more details.) Draw a reference arc (5″) between the 2 arcs.

3. Using the protractor, divide the square into 6 segments: 15°, 30°, 45°, 60°, and 75°. (See Steps 3–5 on pages 21–22 for more details.)

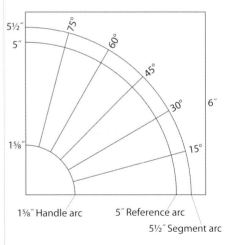

Draw handle, segment, and reference arcs; then divide the square into 6 segments.

4. To create the points, you'll need to determine the midpoint of each segment on the segment arc. You can do this in one of three ways:

- Use the protractor as we did in the Scalloped Fan (page 22).

- Use the compass as described on page 23.

- Draw an X within each segment between the segment and reference arcs. To mark the center point on the segment arc, align the ruler with the handle corner and the intersection; then make a mark on the segment arc. Repeat for each segment.

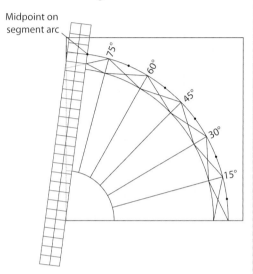

Midpoint on segment arc

Determine and mark the midpoint of each segment.

5. To create the points within each segment, draw 2 lines from the reference arc to the midpoint on the segment arc.

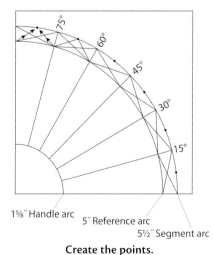

1⅝″ Handle arc
5″ Reference arc
5½″ Segment arc

Create the points.

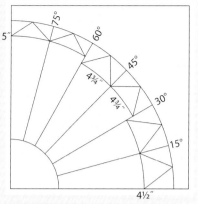

✦✦✦ **Noteworthy** ✦✦✦

The greater the distance between the reference and segment arcs, the higher and sharper the point.

Three different reference arc placements: 4½″, 4¾″, and 5″

FACETED-STYLE FAN BLOCK

This style, which usually has sharper, longer points than previous fan designs, is based on the Mariner's Compass and Sunburst blocks, which we usually see as full-circle designs (i.e., four quarters). For an example, see Marg Gair's beautiful quilt below. The degree of complexity in this design is relative to the number of segments and the placement of the reference arc. In my sampler quilt (page 99), I used two quarters to create a half circle. The variations of fan designs are endless—explore, experiment, and enjoy.

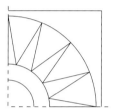

Faceted-Style Fan block

Lady Liberty, 59″ × 59″, designed and machine quilted by Marg Gair, San Ramon, CA. Quilt inspired by a Karen Stone pattern.

TO DRAFT A 4½″ (FINISHED) BLOCK:

1. Draw a 4½″ square.

2. Using the compass, draw the handle arc (1¼″) and segment arc (4¼″), which, in this case, indicates the outer perimeter of the points. (See Step 2 on page 21 for more details.) Draw a reference arc (2″) between the 2 arcs.

3. Using the protractor, divide the square into 4 segments (90° ÷ 4 = 22.5°); then mark dots at 22.5°, 45°, and 67.5°. (See Steps 3–4 on page 22 for more details.) To mark degree dots onto the segment arc, align the edge of the ruler with each degree dot and the handle corner. Do not draw lines; only dots.

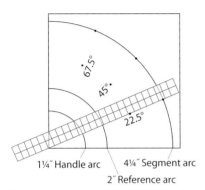

1¼" Handle arc   4¼" Segment arc
2" Reference arc

Draw a square and reference, handle, and segment arcs; then divide the square into 4 segments and mark dots.

4. To make markings on the reference arc at the midpoint of each segment, use the protractor and make a mark 11.25° from the edge. From there, mark every 22.5° (11.25°, 33.75°, 56.25°, 78.75°). To use the compass to find the midpoint, refer to page 23.

5. Connect the markings from the reference arc to the segment arc to create the points and to complete one half of the design, or a quarter of a full circular design.

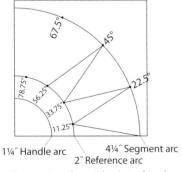

1¼" Handle arc   4¼" Segment arc
2" Reference arc

Determine the midpoint of each segment and create points.

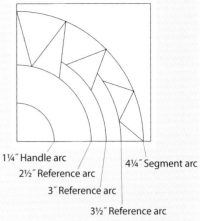

♦♦♦ **Noteworthy** ♦♦♦

The farther the reference arc is from the segment arc, the longer and sharper the points will be.

1¼" Handle arc
2½" Reference arc
3" Reference arc
3½" Reference arc
4¼" Segment arc

Three different reference arc placements: 2½", 3", and 3½"

WINDING WAYS BLOCK

Although this traditional block can often appear contemporary and complex, it is quite simple to draft. When set in a block-to-block fashion, it creates circular designs. Although it consists of only three shapes, it is filled with design and color potential, as is evident in Nancy Elliot MacDonald's stunning quilt below.

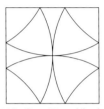

Winding Ways block

Depending on your block size, you might need to tape graph paper together or, if the block is larger than about 12″, employ the yardstick compass.

Black and White, 72″ × 88″, designed, pieced, and machine quilted by Nancy Elliot MacDonald, Carmichael, CA.

1. Choose a block size and draw a 9-square grid of that size on graph paper.

2. Find the center of each square by lightly drawing a line across each square diagonally in both directions. The intersection is the center mark.

3. Place the point of the compass at the center of the center square and expand the compass so the pencil reaches the center of an adjacent square. Draw a circle.

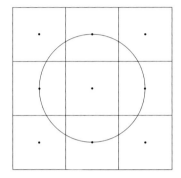

Draw a 9-square grid, find the center of each square, and draw a circle.

4. Without changing the distance of the compass, place the point of the compass at the center of an adjacent square; the compass pencil should reach the center of another square. Draw another circle. Repeat for each square (7 more times) for a total of 9 circles. The center of every square is a pivot point from which to draw a circle. The center square becomes the pattern for your block. There are only 3 template shapes: A, B, and C.

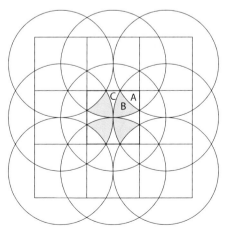

Draw 9 circles (total) to create the pattern.

EQUILATERAL TRIANGLE

An equilateral triangle is one in which all three sides measure the same and in which each side is connected to the other at a 60° angle. Although many quilt patterns use equilateral triangles, the pattern that first comes to mind is 1000 Pyramids, a time-honored traditional quilt pattern that uses only this one shape

Equilateral triangle

(see Linda Cockrell's wonderful quilt below). Any size equilateral triangle is easily drafted from a circle. To know the size of the circle to begin with, you must first decide the size of each side of the equilateral triangle. Let's choose 1½″ per side. The measurement of each triangle side (1½″) is also the radius of the beginning circle, which means the diameter of the circle is 3″ (diameter is the circle size, or twice the radius).

Thousand Pyramids, 24″ × 29″, designed, pieced, and hand quilted by Linda Cockrell, owned by author.

TO DRAFT A 1½″ (FINISHED) EQUILATERAL TRIANGLE:

1. Use your compass to draw a 3″ circle (1½″ radius; see page 19). The center of the circle is point C. Keep the compass at this setting.

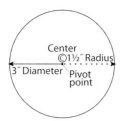

Draw a circle.

2. Place the pivot point anywhere on the circle line, without changing the size of the compass.

3. Swivel the pencil to make a mark over the circle (A).

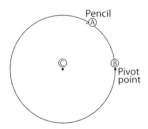

Move the compass pivot point to mark the circle line.

4. Place the pivot point where the pencil just was—again, without changing the size of the compass.

5. Swivel the pencil to make a mark on the circle (B).

6. Draw connecting lines from A to B, A to C, and B to C to create a 1½″ equilateral triangle.

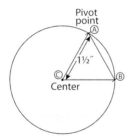

1½″ Equilateral triangle

60° DIAMOND

A 60° diamond is very easy to draft and a natural progression from the equilateral triangle. It is the size and shape of two equilateral triangles. First read through the directions to draft an equilateral triangle (pages 27–28).

To draft a 1½″ (finished) 60° diamond:

1. Follow Steps 1–6 on pages 27–28.

2. Place the pivot point at B and swivel the pencil to make another mark on the circle line (D).

3. Connect B to D and D to C to create the 1½″ 60° diamond.

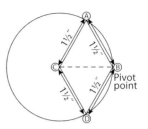

Move the pivot point to B and swivel to make a mark on the circle line.

HEXAGONS

A hexagon is a six-sided shape that offers a multitude of design possibilities. The most common use of this humble shape is that of the familiar Grandmother's Flower Garden. Add to that—with stars, boxes, buildings, or baby blocks, to name a few—and you have a fountain of creative, sophisticated designs to develop from this shape. When using the hexagon for designing, consider its orientation (the point at the top or the side at the top) and know that it will not be square when corners are added. You must add strip(s) to one or two sides of the hexagon to square it (page 32). All six sides of the hexagon measure the same as the radius of the beginning circle.

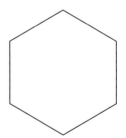

Hexagon positioned with points at the top and bottom

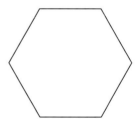

Hexagon positioned with straight sides at the top and bottom

TO DRAFT A 3″ (FINISHED) HEXAGON:

Option 1

1. Using the compass, draw a 3″ circle.

2. Draw a line through the center of the circle, labeling where the ends of the line touch the circle (A and B).

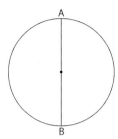

Draw a circle with a line through the center.

3. Using the compass, draw a half-circle: Place the pivot point of the compass at A and the pencil at the center of the circle. Draw the half-circle from one side of the circle to the other.

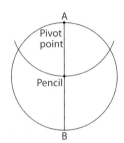

Draw a half-circle.

4. Repeat Step 3 from the B pivot point.

5. Connect the 6 intersections around the circle to create the hexagon. Evaluate and erase all unnecessary lines, leaving only seamlines.

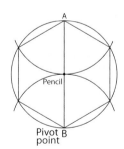

Connect the intersections.

Option 2

1. Using your compass, draw a 3″ circle.

2. Without changing the size of the compass, move the pivot point from the center to anywhere on the circle line. Swivel the pencil to make a mark over the circle line.

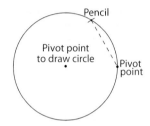

Draw a circle and mark the points.

3. Move the pivot point of the compass to the pencil mark on the circle line. Swivel the pencil to make a second mark on the circle. Repeat this process until you have 6 marks on the circle.

4. Connect the 6 marks to create a hexagon.

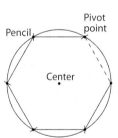

Make 6 marks and connect them to create a hexagon.

BABY BLOCKS

Baby Blocks, or Tumbling Blocks as they are sometimes referred to, are a familiar, traditional design that relies on consistent value placement of light, medium, and dark to effectively achieve a three-dimensional look. It is developed by first drafting a hexagon and then dividing it into three 60° diamonds. See a wonderful variation of this block in *Sampler Supreme* (page 99).

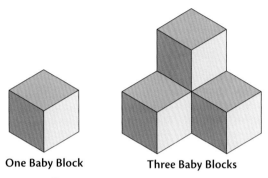

One Baby Block   Three Baby Blocks

TO DRAFT A 3″ (FINISHED) BLOCK:

1. Follow the steps on page 29 to draft a 3″ hexagon, using Option 1 or Option 2.

2. Label and connect 3 hexagon corners (A, B, and C) to the center to create three 1½″ 60° diamonds.

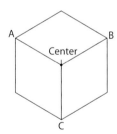

Draw a hexagon and connect the corners to the center.

♦♦♦♦♦♦ Noteworthy ♦♦♦♦♦♦

You only need to make one diamond template to construct this block.

3-DIMENSIONAL HEXAGON BOX BLOCK

I was inspired to make this block by a fabric design that appeared to have three-dimensional boxes on it. My challenge was to create a three-dimensional look through value placement. My initial mock-up used three values of one color. I then decided to try three colors, with three values of each color. One of many lessons I learned was that the degree of light, medium, and dark must be the same for each of the three colors. I thought this would be a good block not only to make but to draft as well. The pattern for my block is on page 103.

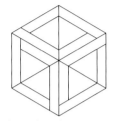

3-Dimensional Hexagon Box

TO DRAFT A 3″ (FINISHED) BOX:

1. Draft a 3″ hexagon (Option 1, page 29) by starting with a 3″ circle, orientated as illustrated. Divide it into 6 equilateral triangles by connecting all opposite points through the center.

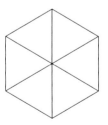

Draft a 3″ hexagon and divide it into 6 equilateral triangles.

2. Draw 2 lines to create a ¼″ border on 2 sides of 1 triangle. This block is made using templates A, B, and C. Repeat in all 6 equilateral triangles.

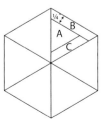

Add ¼″ border to 2 sides of the triangle.

6-POINTED STAR #1 BLOCK

Six-Pointed Star blocks are a common patchwork design that is developed by drafting six 60° diamonds within a hexagon. This star (#1) aligns the points of the star with the midpoints of the sides of the hexagon. Six-Pointed Star #2 (at right) aligns the points of the star with the points of the hexagon.

❖❖❖❖❖❖ **Noteworthy** ❖❖❖❖❖❖

The drafting sequence for both star styles is the same for both hexagon orientations.

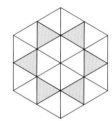

6-Pointed Star #1 block

TO DRAFT A 3″ (FINISHED) BLOCK:

1. Draft a 3″ hexagon positioned with one point at the top and bottom (Option 1, page 29).

2. With a regular pencil, connect opposite corners through the center to create 6 equilateral triangles.

3. With a red pencil, connect opposite midpoints.

4. With a blue pencil, connect every other midpoint to create a blue triangle.

5. With a green pencil, connect the remaining three midpoints to create a green triangle.

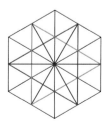

Draft 6-Pointed Star #1 with *hexagon points* on the top and bottom and star points aligned with the midpoint of the hexagon's sides.

6. Erase all unnecessary lines, leaving only seamlines.

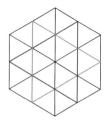

6-Pointed Star #1; after drafting, erase any unnecessary lines.

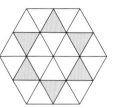

Star #1 rotated with the *hexagon sides* at the top and bottom

6-POINTED STAR #2 BLOCK

Six-Pointed Star blocks are a common patchwork design developed by drafting six 60° diamonds within a hexagon. This star (#2) aligns the points of the star with the points of the hexagon. Six-Pointed Star #1 (at left) aligns the points of the star with the midpoint of the sides of the hexagon.

❖❖❖❖❖❖ **Noteworthy** ❖❖❖❖❖❖

The drafting sequence for both star styles is the same for both hexagon orientations.

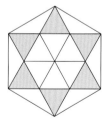

6-Pointed Star #2 block

TO DRAFT A 3″ (FINISHED) BLOCK:

1. Draw a 3″ hexagon positioned with a point at the top and bottom (Option 1, page 29).

2. With a regular pencil, connect the top corner with the 2 lower corners and then connect the lower 2 corners to create a triangle.

3. With a red pencil, connect the lower corner with the 2 upper corners and then connect the upper 2 corners to create a red triangle.

4. With a blue pencil, connect the 6 intersections, which were created by the 2 overlaid triangles, to the center.

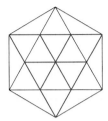

Draft 6-Pointed Star #2 with the *hexagon points* at the top and bottom and star points aligned with the hexagon points.

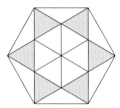

Star #2 rotated with *hexagon sides* at the top and bottom

MAKING HEXAGON BLOCKS SQUARE

When you put corners on any hexagon design, you will have a rectangle, not a square. If you want a square block, you must add 1 strip (Option 1) or 2 strips (Option 2) to the long sides of the block.

Measure the length and width finished and subtract the smaller number from the larger. The difference is what you need to add to your block to make it square. For example, if you have a 6″ hexagon, it will measure 6″ × 5³/₁₆″. The difference between 6″ and 5³/₁₆″ is ¹³/₁₆″. To make your block square, you have one of three options.

Option 1

Add one strip the width of the difference plus ½″ (for the seam allowance) by the length of the block to one long side of the block.

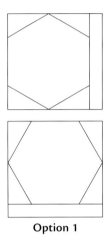

Option 1

Option 2

Divide the difference in half, add ½″ for seam allowance, cut two strips this width × the length of the block, and add them to the two long sides of the block.

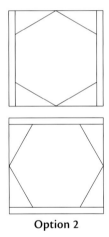

Option 2

Option 3

Cut the strip (or strips) you add wider than needed; then trim the block to the size you need.

DRAFTING FOR THE CREATIVE QUILTER

5-POINTED STAR BLOCK

Whenever I think of a five-pointed star, I always think of the Texas star on the state flag. It is simple to draft and, like most patchwork, has design potential as well.

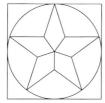

5-Pointed Star block

◆◆◆◆◆ **Noteworthy** ◆◆◆◆◆

I use a round protractor when dividing circles into equal sections. Align the crosshairs with the center so that the two 90° marks run north and south and the 180° and 360° marks run east and west. I begin marking from the 360°/0° mark and work clockwise.

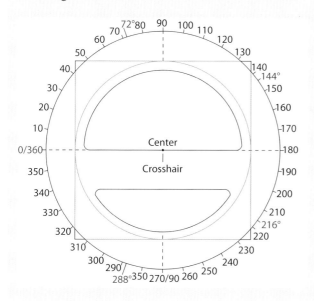

TO DRAFT A 6˝ (FINISHED) BLOCK:

1. Draw a 6˝ square.

2. Using a compass, draw a 6˝ circle inside the square.

3. To divide the circle into 5 equal divisions, divide 360° by 5 (72°). You will mark around the circle every 72°. Figure out your numbers first and write them down. Using the round protractor and adding 72, you will mark at 72°, 144°, 216°, 288°, and 360°.

4. Transfer the angle markings to the circle line by aligning the edge of the ruler with both the center of the circle and one of the degree markings. Place a dot on the circle line next to the ruler edge. Repeat to mark the remaining 4 increments.

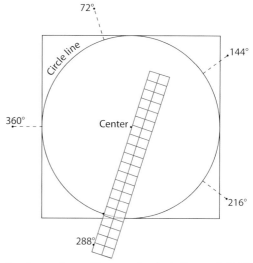

Transfer the angle markings to the circle line and divide the circle into 5 equal divisions.

5. Position your drawing so one point is in the middle of the top line of the square. On my drawing, this point is at the 0/360° mark. Starting here and working clockwise, number the markings 1–5. Using your ruler, connect 1 to 3, 3 to 5, 5 to 2, 2 to 4, and 4 to 1.

6. Connect the 5 corners of the center pentagon to the center of the circle (shown in red).

7. Erase all unnecessary lines, leaving only seamlines.

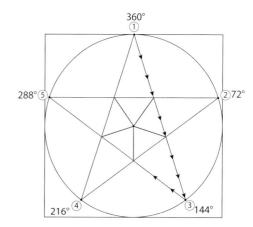

Number the markings 1–5 and connect with lines.

10-POINTED STAR BLOCK

A 10-Pointed Star block is a progression of the 5-Pointed Star block (page 33) and has huge potential for design. Once this star is drafted, it is up to you to decide which lines to keep and which to erase. This is also the time to add design lines. Here I describe how I drafted the 6″ 10-Pointed Star block in the sampler project quilt on page 99.

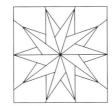

Sampler Block—10-Pointed Star

TO DRAFT A 6″ (FINISHED) BLOCK:

1. Draw a 6″ square. Using a compass, draw a 6″ circle inside the square.

2. Using the round protractor, divide the circle by 10 (360° ÷ 10 = 36°). (See page 33 for proper positioning.) Working clockwise from 360°/0°, mark every 36° at the edge of the protractor (36°, 72°, 108°, 144°, 180°, 216°, 252°, 288°, 324°, 360°).

3. Transfer each angle marking to the circle line by aligning the ruler edge with both the center of the circle and the angle marking (page 33).

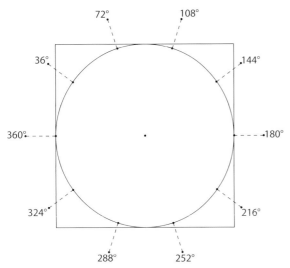

Transfer each angle marking to the circle line.

4. Position the paper so that the point touching the middle of the top line is the 360° mark. Working clock-wise, number each angle marking 1–10. Connect 1 to 5, 5 to 9, 9 to 3, 3 to 7, and 7 to 1.

5. With a red pencil, connect 2 to 6, 6 to 10, 10 to 4, 4 to 8, and 8 to 2.

6. With a blue pencil, connect through the center 1 to 6, 2 to 7, 3 to 8, 4 to 9, and 5 to 10.

7. Add additional design lines or erase unnecessary lines as needed, leaving only seamlines.

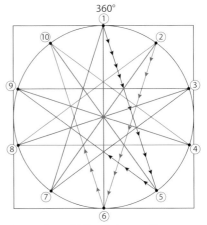

With a point at the middle of the top line, connect angle markings to create a star.

DRAFTING FOR THE CREATIVE QUILTER

DOUBLE WEDDING RING

Diana McClun and Laura Nownes have graciously and generously given me permission to offer their instructions from their book *Quilts Galore* for drafting one variation of a Double Wedding Ring block in any size you choose. In 1995, I used these instructions to draft a small double wedding ring quilt using a 6″ ring. I am honored and grateful to be able to share them with you here, exactly as they appeared in their book. Any updating of techniques or tools that could be applied to them is at your own discretion.

If you are like most quilters, you do not have the proper drafting tools required to make large circles. The small compasses we are all familiar with do not have enough expansion to make a large ring. But you can easily make your own tool with a strip of template plastic and push pins.

Presented here is only one of the many variations of the Double Wedding Ring. This variation forms a circle, whereas others are more oblong. After you become familiar with the technique, you may wish to vary the width of the pieced arcs or the number of segments within them.

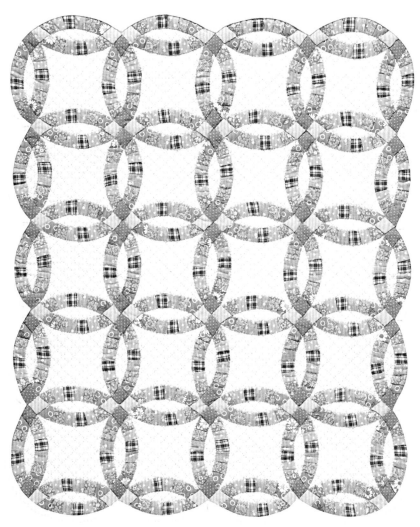

Double Wedding Ring, 6″ Rings, 18″ × 22″, designed, pieced, and hand quilted by the author.

TO DRAFT AN 18″ (FINISHED) DOUBLE WEDDING RING BLOCK:

1. Determine the size ring you would like to make, for example, 18″.

2. Divide your ring size by 2, for example, 9″.

3. Using your large C-Thru ruler and lead pencil, mark a square of this size on the graph paper.

4. Mark the corners A, B, C, and D, exactly as shown in the diagram.

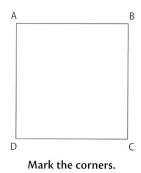

Mark the corners.

5. Divide your square size by 5 and use this measurement to mark a distance from point B to point E, from point B to point F, from point D to point G, and from point D to point H, exactly as shown in the diagram.

Helpful hint: If your block size is not evenly divisible by 5, round off to the nearest eighth. Use the chart below for help. For example, 9 ÷ 5 = 1.8; 0.8 is closest to 0.75, so use 1.75, or 1¾.

0.125 = ⅛

0.25 = ¼

0.375 = ⅜

0.5 = ½

0.625 = ⅝

0.75 = ¾

0.875 = ⅞

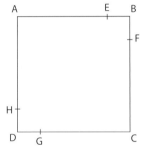

Divide the square size and mark the points.

6. Cut a strip of template plastic 1″ wide by at least 1″ larger than one side of your square.

7. Place a push pin through the center of one of the short ends approximately ¼″ from the edge, exactly as shown in the diagram.

Insert push pin here.

Plastic template strip

Place a push pin.

8. Lay your graph paper over the piece of cardboard (or rotary cutting mat to stabilize point of compass). Then secure the push pin and plastic template strip at point A. Make sure that the plastic template strip lies flat against the graph paper.

9. Adjust the plastic template strip so that it lies over point E. Then use the permanent marking pen to indicate this point with a dot on the plastic template strip. This point will be used for constructing the inner arc.

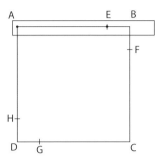

Mark point E on the template.

10. Without removing the push pin, rotate the plastic template strip toward yourself until it lies over point F. Then use the permanent pen to indicate this point with a dot on the plastic template strip. This point will be used for constructing the outer arc.

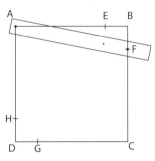

Mark point F on the template.

11. Use the other push pin to pierce through the plastic at each of the 2 dots. Push the pin through as far as it will go, as the holes must be large enough to accommodate the tip of the pencil. Remove pin.

12. With the plastic strip and push pin still secure at point A, place the tip of your pencil into the hole made for the inner arc. Starting at point E, rotate the pencil and plastic template strip around to point H, forming an arc, exactly as shown in

the diagram. **Helpful hint:** Point H is simply a checkpoint. It is the end point of the arc.

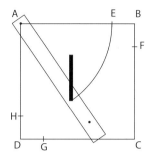

Rotate pencil to form an arc.

13. Next, place the tip of your pencil into the hole on the plastic template strip for making the outer arc. Starting at point F, rotate the pencil and plastic strip around to point G, forming an arc, exactly as shown in the diagram. **Helpful hint:** Point G is simply a checkpoint. It is the end point of the arc.

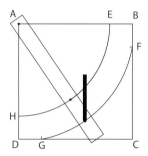

Rotate pencil to form an arc.

14. Remove the push pin from point A and secure it with the plastic template strip at point C.

15. Repeat Steps 12 and 13 to draw an inner arc from point F to point G and an outer arc from point E to point H, exactly as shown in the diagram.

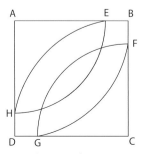

Draw inner and outer arcs.

16. Lay your protractor over the square, exactly as shown in the diagram. Line DC should be in line with the 0° marking, and line BC should be in line with the 90° marking.

17. Use your pencil to mark points at 25°, 35°, 45°, 55°, and 65°, exactly as shown in the diagram.

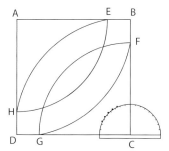

Position the protractor and mark degree markings.

18. Position your C-Thru ruler to intersect with the 25° mark and point C and beyond the farthest arc. Then, draw a straight line between the 2 farthest arcs, exactly as shown in the diagram.

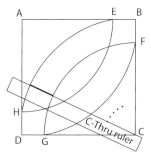

Draw a line between 2 arcs.

19. Next, position your C-Thru ruler to intersect with the 35° mark and point C, and mark a straight line in the upper arc. Repeat this step with the 45°, 55°, and 65° markings to complete the shapes within the arc section, exactly as shown in the diagram.

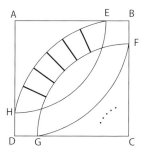

Complete the shapes within the arc.

20. Repeat Step 16 in the upper left-hand corner of the square. It may be helpful to rotate your graph paper so that point A is in the lower right-hand corner.

21. Repeat Steps 17–19, placing the protractor at point A, to mark straight lines in the opposite arc section.

22. Notice that the line joining the post to the end of the pieced arc is curved. When sewing these 2 pieces together, the curves will be opposing and will require some maneuvering to sew smoothly. You can easily avoid this situation if you mark straight lines from the tip of the melon section to points E and F, exactly as shown in the diagram. Do this again at the opposite set of posts.

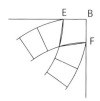

Straighten the curved lines.

23. Use the eraser to eliminate the points made in Steps 17 and 21.

24. At this point you have drafted one-quarter of the ring and all of the shapes required to make the Double Wedding Ring. However, if you would like to draft the entire ring or view the entire pattern, you can repeat the previous steps 3 more times. Or you may choose to trace

the block or make photocopies of it and tape the sections together to form the complete ring, exactly as shown in the diagram. Otherwise, this completes the Double Wedding Ring. There are 5 templates shapes: #1 the inner segments of the pieced arc, #2 and #2R the ends of the pieced arc, #3 the melon shape, #4 the post, and #5 the large background piece. Note that template shape #5 is only one-quarter of the entire shape. To achieve the full shape, the 2 straight sides must be placed on the fold when cutting the fabric shape. Indicate this on the template shape. Do not add seam allowance to these 2 sides when making your plastic template.

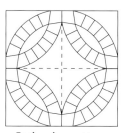

Entire ring pattern

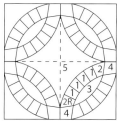

5 template shapes

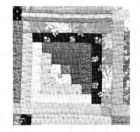

Log Cabin and Pineapple Blocks

LOG CABIN AND COURTHOUSE STEPS BLOCKS

These two time-honored designs continue to be popular today. The components of both a Log Cabin block and a Courthouse Steps block are the same—a center square, or "chimney," with strips, or "logs," added around the chimney.

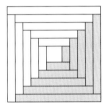 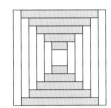

Log Cabin block   **Courthouse Steps block**

The Log Cabin block is usually colored diagonally, with light fabrics on one diagonal half and dark fabrics on the other diagonal half. Any design you can create with half-square triangles, you can create with Log Cabin blocks. The logs are added to the chimney in either a clockwise or a counterclockwise spiral fashion—just be consistent.

Half-square triangle unit

The Courthouse Steps block is colored in diagonal quarters and can be used the same as any quarter-square triangle unit. The logs are added to the top and bottom of the chimney and then to the two sides repeatedly until the block is complete.

Quarter-square triangle unit

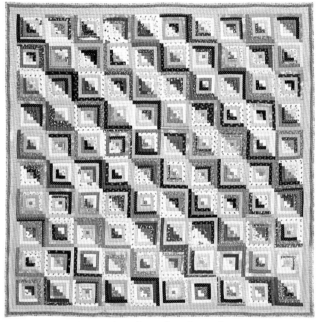

Antique Log Cabin Quilt, 76" × 76", maker unknown.

When designing, you make all the choices. Keep in mind that nothing is written in stone; you can always make changes. If I'm in question about proportion, I usually sketch a block on graph paper to see how it will look before I begin a final draft.

You decide the following:

- Block size

- Center (chimney) size—When drafting from the inside out, I usually make the center either the size of the logs or twice the size of the logs. The center can also be a pieced block or a rectangle or another shape such as a diamond (45° or 60°) or hexagon. Changing the shape of the center square alters the shape of the block.

- Log or strip size—Proportion is important. If you choose a 6″ block, 2″ logs are too wide. I usually stay with ¼″- to 1½″-wide logs.

- Number of logs or strips—Going around the center at least four times is a suggested proportion, though the narrower the strips and the more there are of them, the more color, design, and detail you can create.

- Odd or even number of logs

Drafting the Log Cabin and Courthouse Steps blocks can be done from the outside inward, if a specific block size is needed for a sampler quilt or friendship exchange, or from the inside outward, when block size is not an issue, as perhaps in the case of a repeat block quilt. All the blocks just need to be the same size.

Drafting from the Outside Inward

TO DRAFT A 6″ (FINISHED) BLOCK:

1. For either Log Cabin or Courthouse Steps, draw a 6″ square.

2. In this example, we'll use ½″ logs. Working from the outside inward and on one side at a time, lightly draw grid lines the finished width of the logs apart (½″). Draw as many lines as there are logs (5). The center square (chimney) remains.

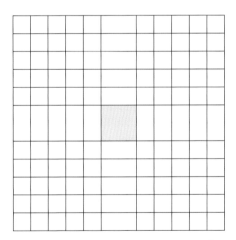

Working inward, add grid lines to create logs.

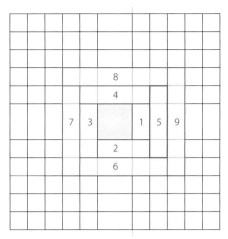

For the Log Cabin block: Work clockwise from the center out, darkening seamlines over the grid in red pencil and numbering the logs 1–20 for the sewing sequence. You could also work counterclockwise instead—just be consistent.

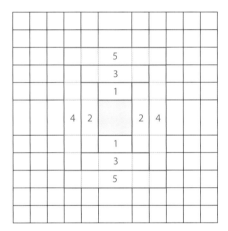

For Courthouse Steps block: Work from the center out, adding logs to the top and bottom, then to the two opposite sides, repeatedly. Number the logs 1–10 (two of each) for the sewing sequence. Odd numbers are the top and bottom logs and even numbers are the side logs.

Drafting from the Inside Outward

1. Draw a square larger than the size you want.

2. Draw a center square within the larger square.

3. Based on either the Log Cabin or the Courthouse Steps design, add logs until you come close to a size you like, checking to be sure you have the same number of logs on each side of the chimney.

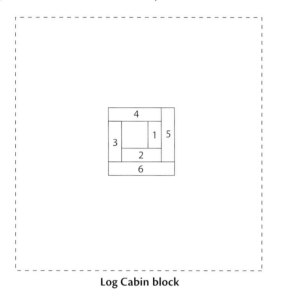

Log Cabin block

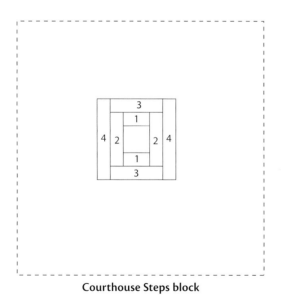

Courthouse Steps block

OFF-CENTER LOG CABIN BLOCK

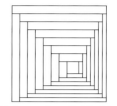

Off-Center Log Cabin block

The Off-Center Log Cabin block is just that—a traditional Log Cabin block with the chimney moved away from center. Multiple blocks sewn together create a somewhat curved design. To see how the block looks when four are joined, place your mirrors (page 91) on the corner where the small logs merge.

There is no specific formula to determine the widths of the logs. Experimentation is a great teacher. I like a 2-to-1 ratio. For example, for a 6″ block, I would choose ½″ and ¼″ logs. The center (or chimney) ends up as a ¾″ square (the total of two logs). The larger the difference between the two log widths, the farther offset the chimney will be. This is a good time to sketch rather than estimate how wide the two different logs should be.

Drafting from the Outside Inward

TO DRAFT A 6″ (FINISHED) BLOCK:

1. Draw a 6″ square.

2. Draw 2 wider logs on one corner, and then draw 2 narrow logs on the opposite corner. The order in which you add them does matter, just be consistent: Add wide/top, wide/left side, narrow/bottom, and then narrow/right side.

Draw a square and add wider and narrower logs.

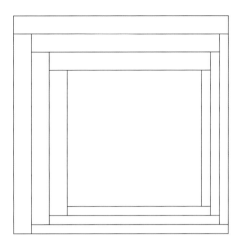

Continue to add logs until you have a center square the size you want. Check to be sure you have the same number of logs on all 4 sides of the block.

Drafting from the Inside Outward

1. You can estimate the size of the center square or add together the finished width of 1 wide and 1 narrow strip. For example, ½″ and ¼″ logs equal a ¾″ center.

2. Draw the 2 narrow logs first, then the 2 wider logs, repeating this sequence until the block is close to the size you want.

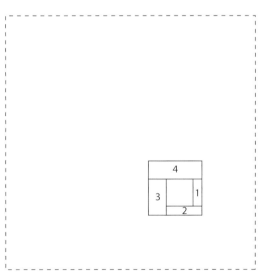

Draw the off-set center square, approximating its position on the paper.

PINEAPPLE BLOCK

Pineapple Quilt, 65″ × 65″, designed, pieced, and machine quilted by Charlene Dakin, Lafayette, CA. Inspired by a Freddy Moran pattern.

Pineapple block

The Pineapple block is a close relative to the Log Cabin and Courthouse Steps blocks (page 38), although its inception was well after the introduction of the Log Cabin. All three blocks are created by adding strips around a center square. Visually the Log Cabin block is divided in half diagonally, the Courthouse Steps block is divided into quarters diagonally, and the Pineapple block is divided into eight sections, with four on the horizontal/vertical planes and four on the diagonal planes.

A common Pineapple block comprises a center square surrounded by five rounds of strips. The center square is twice the size of the strip width. For example, a 1″ center square would be surrounded by ½″ strips. The number of rounds is up to the maker, although five rounds is common because it is visually balanced: Five strips on each side of the center makes 10; and a center that is twice the width of the strip makes 2; so the block is divided equally by 12. If you choose to have 4 strips on either side of the center square, then you would have 10 equal divisions (4 on each side and 2 for the center).

To keep your cutting numbers ruler friendly (down to ⅛″), it is easiest to choose a block size divisible by 3 (3″, 4½″, 6″, 7½″, 9″, and so on).

There are three numbers you need to know when drafting a Pineapple block: the block size, the strip width (the center is twice the strip width), and the number of divisions. Whichever two numbers you choose, you must figure out the third. For example:

If the choice is a **6″ block with 12 divisions,** then you need to **figure out the strip width**. To do so, divide the block size (6″) by the number of divisions (12) to end up with 0.5″, or ½″, strips with a 1″ center.

If the choice is a **6″ block with ¾″ strips**, then you need to **figure out how many divisions** the block will have. To do so, divide the block size (6″) by the strip width (0.75) = 8 divisions, with 3 on each side of the center square and 2 for the center square.

If the choice is **½″ strips and 12 divisions**, then you need to **figure out the block size**. Multiply the number of divisions (12) by the width of the strips (½″) = 6″ block.

Drafting from the Outside Inward

TO DRAFT A 6″ (FINISHED) BLOCK:

1. Draw a 6″ square and divide it in half vertically, horizontally, and diagonally in both directions.

2. Working from the center to each edge, mark six ½″ divisions.

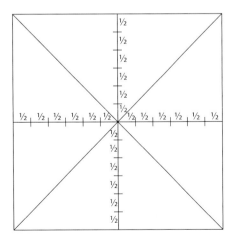

Divide the square and mark divisions.

3. Using a *colored pencil*, draw the center square and 5 concentric squares around the center at the division marks.

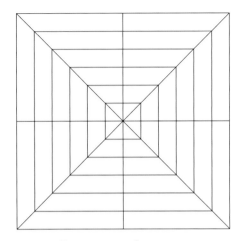

Draw concentric squares.

4. Using your *regular pencil*, draw a square on-point around the center square. Starting from a corner of the original center square, measure and mark 5 increments ½″ along the 4 diagonal lines.

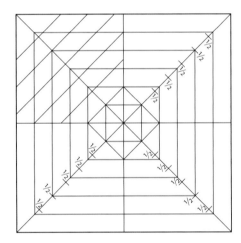

Draw a square on-point and mark ½″ increments.

DRAFTING FOR THE CREATIVE QUILTER

If you have a compass that holds its position well, set the expansion at ½" and place the pivot point on the corner of the center square. Then make a mark over the diagonal line by swiveling the pencil point across the diagonal line. Next, move the pivot point to where your mark and the diagonal line intersect and swivel the pencil point over the diagonal line again. Continue toward the corner and repeat until you have five ½" markings. Check the compass measurement often to be sure it is holding its position.

5. Using a regular lead pencil and a ruler, draw a straight line at each division mark along the diagonal lines, parallel to the side of the center on-point square. To help yourself draw straight parallel lines, position a ruler line exactly over the diagonal line you are working from. You should have 5 parallel lines ½" apart. Repeat for the remaining 3 corners. To check for accuracy, fold the drawing in half horizontally and hold it up to a lightbox or window. Then fold it in half vertically and check again. Then do the same for each diagonal.

6. To create the trapezoid shapes, erase the original horizontal, vertical, and diagonal lines and all right angle lines and corners to reveal the 6" Pineapple block.

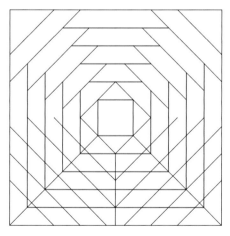

Erase lines to create shapes.

Now that you have an understanding of how to draft the common Pineapple block, it will be easy to make changes to customize your block. Experiment with strip width, corner size, and center size. Try adding a square on-point within the center square, or remove the original square to reveal a square on-point for the center. Refer to the bibliography (page 127) for references on this versatile, graphic, traditional block.

Detail of *Pineapple Quilt*, page 41

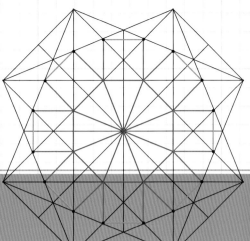

8-Pointed Star Blocks

Most quilters love stars. Designs in the 8-pointed star category are some of the most beautiful and graceful designs; I have been focused on, fascinated with, and challenged by them since the early 1980s when I made my third quilt. It was a Lone Star design with a pieced border (remember, ignorance is bliss sometimes) made to fit on our queen-size water bed! Designs in this category often have the potential to carry an entire quilt.

The 8-pointed star drafting category is based on eight 45° divisions of a circle (360° ÷ 8 = 45°). Although the circle is not always apparent in the underlying structure, a circle may be added to any block to create additional design lines.

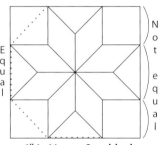

6″ LeMoyne Star block

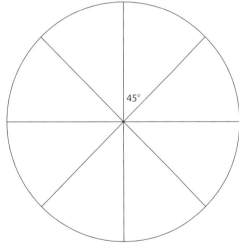

8 divisions of a circle

The three divisions along the edge of an 8-pointed star are not equal, though the distance between the star points is equal. The distance between the star points is also the same as the middle division of the block and the diagonal distance across the corner square.

Recognizing designs based on the 8-pointed star drafting category takes some practice. The following is a list of characteristics to look for. However, not all characteristics are always in every block.

CHARACTERISTICS OF 8-POINTED STAR DESIGNS

- The divisions along the edge are not equal.

- There are 45° diamonds in the design.

- Eight 45° seams radiate from the center outward.

- The distance between the star points is equal to the middle divisions on the block's edge.

- You can recognize an octagon (8 equal sides) in the design.

- Angles in the design are either 90° or 45°.

DRAFTING FOR THE CREATIVE QUILTER

There will be times, depending on the complexity of your design, when you will have drawn a lot of lines. Use different-colored pencils to help clarify the drafting process. The initial lines you draw, based on the basic structure, are construction lines needed to draft and create the design. Construction lines are not always seamlines. You will erase all unnecessary lines to create the design, and then shade the needed template shapes. Because many of the following designs are symmetrical, you only need to draft one-eighth or one-quarter of the design to create the necessary template shapes.

Once you get going, you will see the sense of things; you will see repetition of diamonds, 90° and/or 45° angles, octagons, and so on. The lights will go on, I promise you. If you find that you love 8-pointed star designs, then keep going and discover how to make your own beautiful 8-Pointed Star blocks in any size you choose (the exercises in this book will draft 6″ blocks).

You will need graph paper, a compass, a pencil, and a ruler.

BASIC UNDERLYING STRUCTURE

This structure is the stepping stone to an abundance of 8-pointed star drafting designs. Not all are stars, and yet all share a common bond of shape, space, and angles.

TO DRAFT A 6″ (FINISHED) BASIC UNDERLYING STRUCTURE:

1. Draw a 6″ square. Divide the square in half diagonally in both directions and then vertically and horizontally.

2. Using your compass, place the pivot point at a corner and expand the pencil to the exact center.

3. Leaving the pivot point at the corner and holding the compass position, swivel the pencil to lightly mark the 2 lines that extend from that corner.

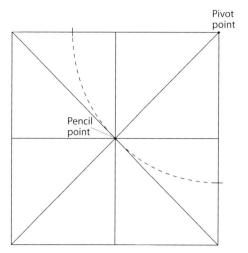

Divide the square, expand the compass from one corner to the center, and mark 2 lines that extend from that corner.

4. Repeat Steps 2 and 3 for the remaining corners. Label the marks A and B and erase the curved lines.

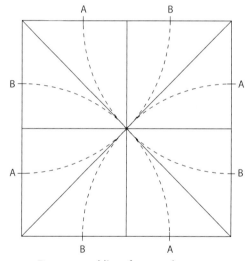

Draw curved lines from each corner.

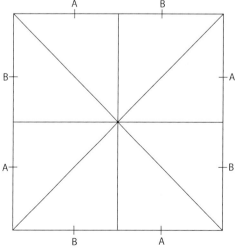

**BASIC UNDERLYING STRUCTURE:
Label marks A and B and erase the curved lines.**

Create this basic underlying structure to draft numerous 8-pointed star drafting designs. You will connect the A's and B's in different ways, depending on your design. Following are five different ways to connect the A's and B's. Often designs will require a combination of these methods. Carefully follow the step-by-step instructions for each design you are drafting.

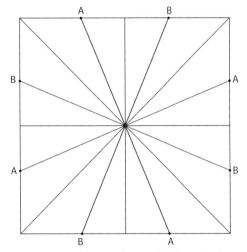

Connect A to A and B to B diagonally through the center.

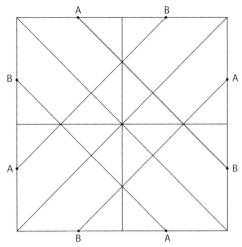

Connect A to every second B, working clockwise.

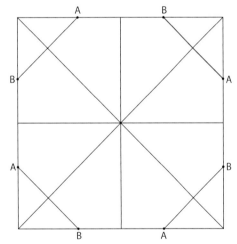

Connect A to B diagonally at the corners.

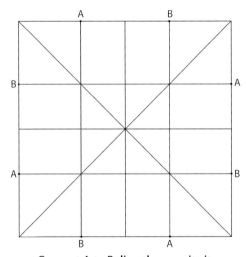

Connect A to B directly opposite it.

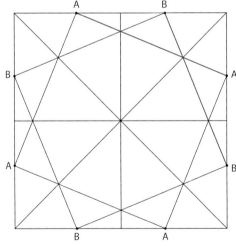

Connect each A to the next A and each B to the next B, starting from the top edge and working clockwise.

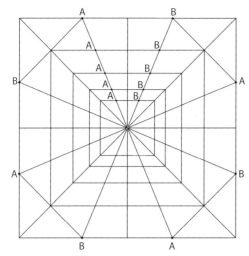

The A and B division along the outside edges of the square continues when you draw concentric smaller squares inside the original one.

As you draft the following blocks, you may need to draft either a smaller concentric square or smaller 8-pointed star design. You will notice that the underlying structure you begin with, and which includes the A and B divisions, continues along those 45° angles into the center. Along any square's edge, the A and B divisions continue, so you can draft an 8-Pointed Star block quite easily.

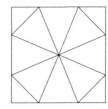

Kaleidoscope Block

The simplest design to begin with is, in fact, not a star but has some characteristics of an 8-pointed star drafting category, see page 44—unequal divisions on its edge, eight 45° angles radiating from the center outward, etc.

TO DRAFT A 6″ (FINISHED) BLOCK:

1. Draw a 6″ square and the Basic Underlying Structure (see page 45).

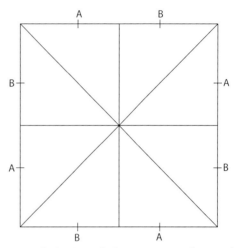

Draw the basic underlying structure (page 45).

2. Connect A to B at the 4 corners. Connect A to A diagonally through the center and B to B diagonally through the center.

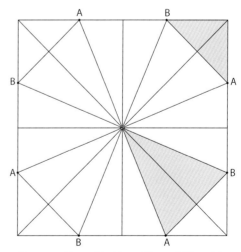

Connect A's to B's, A's to A's, and B's to B's.

3. Erase all unnecessary lines, leaving only seamlines.

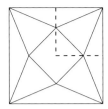

World Without End Block

A World Without End block is created by rotating the four quarters of a Kaleidoscope block 180 degrees.

TO DRAFT A 6˝ (FINISHED) BLOCK:

1. Draw a 6″ Basic Underlying Structure (page 45).

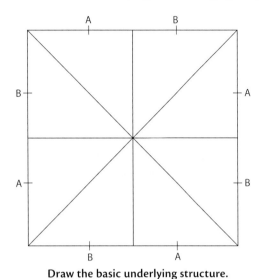

Draw the basic underlying structure.

2. With a **red** pencil, connect each A to the second B, working clockwise from the top A. This creates the on-point square.

3. With a **blue** pencil, connect each outside corner to 2 adjoining corners of the red center square; repeat 3 more times.

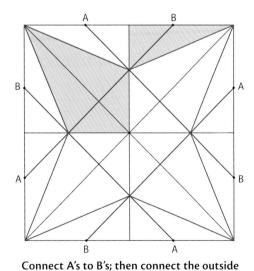

Connect A's to B's; then connect the outside corners to the red corners.

4. Erase all unnecessary lines, leaving only seamlines.

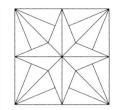

Mother's Delight Block

This block takes World Without End (at left) just a couple of steps further.

TO DRAFT A 6˝ (FINISHED) BLOCK:

1. Draft a 6″ World Without End block (at left); do not erase any lines.

2. Where the horizontal and vertical lines meet the outside edge of the block, label those 1. Where the diagonal lines intersect with the side of the red square, label those 2.

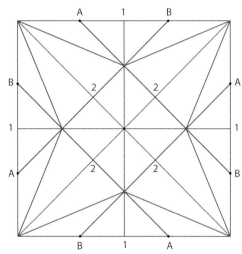

Draft a World Without End block; then label the lines and intersections.

3. With an **orange** pencil, connect each 1 to two 2's.

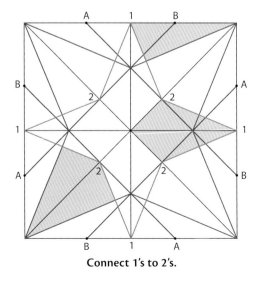

Connect 1's to 2's.

4. Erase all unnecessary lines, leaving only seamlines.

DRAFTING FOR THE CREATIVE QUILTER

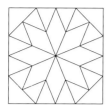

Evening Star Block

This is one of many 8-pointed stars that stand on one point instead of on two.

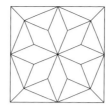

Evening Star Variation Block

A few lines added to an Evening Star make this block a little more formal.

TO DRAFT A 6″ (FINISHED) BLOCK:

1. Draft a 6″ Kaleidoscope block (page 47); do not erase any lines.

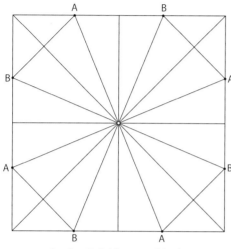

Draft a Kaleidoscope block.

2. Where the horizontal and vertical lines meet the outer edge, label 1, 3, 5, and 7, starting from the top and working clockwise.

3. Where the corner diagonal lines intersect with each corner's AB diagonal line, label 2, 4, 6, and 8, starting at the upper right corner and working clockwise.

4. With a **red** pencil, connect 1 to 4 to 7 to 2 to 5 to 8 to 3 to 6 to 1.

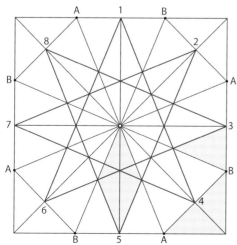

Label the horizontal, vertical, and diagonal lines.
Connect the numbers.

5. Erase all unnecessary lines, leaving only seamlines.

TO DRAFT A 6″ (FINISHED) BLOCK:

1. Draft a 6″ Evening Star block (at left); do not erase any lines.

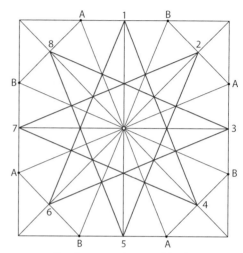

Draft an Evening Star block.

2. With a **blue** pencil, connect points 1 through 8 and back to 1, sequentially.

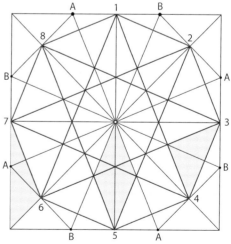

Connect 1–8 and back to 1.

3. Erase all unnecessary lines, leaving only seamlines.

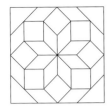

Rolling Star Block

Although this block has only three shapes, it appears more complex than it really is. Both diamonds are the same size.

TO DRAFT A 6″ (FINISHED) BLOCK:

1. Draft a 6″ Kaleidoscope block (page 47); do not erase any lines.

2. Where the horizontal and vertical lines meet the edge of the block, label those 1, 3, 5, and 7, starting at the top and working clockwise.

3. Where the diagonal lines intersect at each corner, label those intersections 2, 4, 6, and 8.

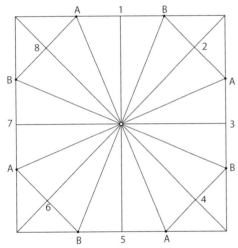

**Draft a Kaleidoscope block. Connect A's and B's.
Label the horizontal, vertical, and diagonal lines.**

4. With a **red** pencil, connect 1 to 3 to 5 to 7 to 1 to create an on-point square.

5. With a **blue** pencil, connect 2 to 4 to 6 to 8 to 2 to create a square.

◆◆◆◆◆◆ Noteworthy ◆◆◆◆◆◆

Where the red and blue lines intersect, another layer of A and B points is created (basic structure); label those intersections A and B. Refer to page 45 for clarification, if necessary.

6. To create the square you need, align your ruler as if to connect a new A to a new B directly opposite each other. Use a **green** pencil to draw in the sides of the squares.

7. With an **orange** pencil, work clockwise from the top to connect each new A to a second new B. This creates the center diamonds, which are exactly the same size as the outer-edge diamonds.

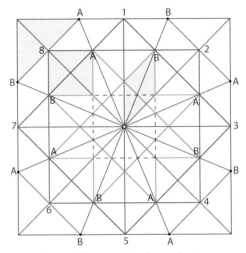

Use a different color for each step.

8. Erase all unnecessary lines, leaving only seamlines.

DRAFTING FOR THE CREATIVE QUILTER

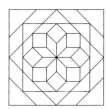

Star and Chains Block

This block is similar to Rolling Star (page 50), but it has an additional layer of diamonds around the center star. You will also be labeling additional intersections, so watch the illustrations carefully and move slowly.

TO DRAFT A 6″ (FINISHED) BLOCK:

1. Draft a 6″ Kaleidoscope block (page 47); do not erase any lines.

2. Where the horizontal and vertical lines meet the outside edge, label those 1, 3, 5, and 7, working clockwise from the top.

3. Where the diagonal lines intersect at the 4 corners, label those intersections 2, 4, 6, and 8, working clockwise from the upper right corner.

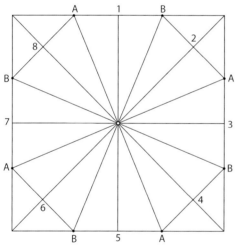

Draft a Kaleidoscope block. Then label the horizontal, vertical, and diagonal lines.

4. With a **red** pencil, connect 1 to 3 to 5 to 7 to 1 to create an on-point square.

5. With a **blue** pencil, connect 2 to 4 to 6 to 8 to 2 to create a square (you have now also created 2 triangles and a diamond).

6. Inside the blue square, where the horizontal and vertical lines meet the blue line, label those 9, 11, 13, and 15.

7. Where the diagonal lines intersect the **red** line, label those 10, 12, 14, and 16.

8. With an **orange** pencil, connect 9 to 11 to 13 to 15 to 9 to create a second, smaller on-point square.

9. With a **green** pencil, connect 10 to 12 to 14 to 16 to 10 to create another square.

10. The intersection where the orange and green lines intersect on each of the 4 sides of the green square divides the square into the basic underlying structure. (Refer to page 45 for clarification.)

11. To draft the small inner star, start on top and work clockwise as you connect each A to an opposite B and to the second B. To lessen the confusion of so many lines, connect 1 A to 2 B's and then turn the paper a quarter turn and repeat. Note that the 2 smaller diamonds are the same size.

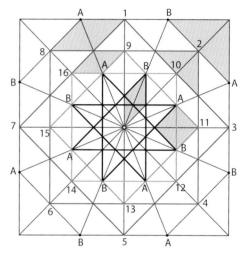

Use a different color for each step.

12. Erase all unnecessary lines, leaving only seamlines.

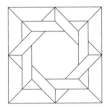

Interlocking Squares Block

This is one of my favorite blocks. It has nothing to do with a star, although the center octagon shape is already set up to draft one inside (see pages 31–32).

TO DRAFT A 6″ (FINISHED) BLOCK:

1. Draft a 6″ Kaleidoscope block (page 47); do not erase any lines or letters.

2. Where the horizontal and vertical lines meet the outer edge, label those 1, 3, 5, and 7.

3. Where the AB diagonal lines at the corners intersect with the block's diagonal line, label those intersections 2, 4, 6, and 8.

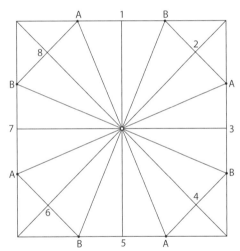

Draft a Kaleidoscope block; then label the horizontal, vertical, and diagonal lines.

4. With a **red** pencil, connect 1 to 3 to 5 to 7 to 1 to create an on-point square.

5. With a **blue** pencil, connect 2 to 4 to 6 to 8 to 2 to create a square, extending the lines to the edge.

6. Where the horizontal and vertical lines intersect the blue line, label those intersections 9, 11, 13, and 15.

7. Where the block's diagonal line intersects the side of the on-point square, label those intersections 10, 12, 14, and 16.

8. With a **red** pencil, connect 9 to 11 to 13 to 15 to 9 to create a second, smaller on-point square.

9. With a **green** pencil, connect 10 to 12 to 14 to 16 to 10 to create a second, small square.

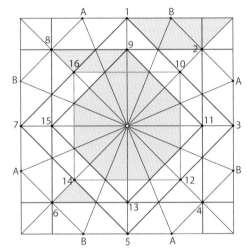

Use a different color for each step.

10. Erase all unnecessary lines, leaving only seamlines.

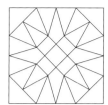

North Carolina Star Block

As I researched blocks, this one was new to me, but easy to draft and lovely.

TO DRAFT A 6″ (FINISHED) BLOCK:

1. Draft a 6″ Kaleidoscope block (page 47); do not erase any lines.

2. Moving clockwise and starting at the top edge, connect each A to the B directly opposite it, as well as to a second B diagonally across the square. This creates a large LeMoyne Star.

3. Label the intersection inside each diamond 2. I have drawn the large star in red and circled the intersections so you can more easily see them, though there is no need for you to do so.

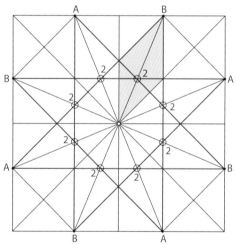

Draft a Kaleidoscope block; connect the A's to the B's and label the intersections within the diamonds.

4. Where the horizontal and vertical lines meet the block edge, label those 1.

5. Where the diagonal line going toward the corner intersects the AB diagonal across the corner, label those 3.

6. To create the center on-point square and four rectangles, use a **red** pencil to connect two 2's four times.

7. With a **blue** pencil, connect two 2's to a 1 four times.

8. With an **orange** pencil, connect two 2's to a 3 and connect the 2's to each other 4 times.

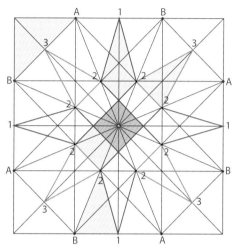

Label the horizontal and vertical lines and intersections. Use different colors to connect the points.

9. Erase all unnecessary lines, leaving only seamlines.

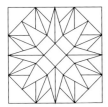

North Carolina Star Variation Block

To draft a North Carolina Star Variation block, you will keep the eight points of the initial 8-pointed star you drafted when connecting the A's and B's.

TO DRAFT A 6″ (FINISHED) BLOCK:

1. Draft a 6″ North Carolina Star (page 53); do not erase any lines.

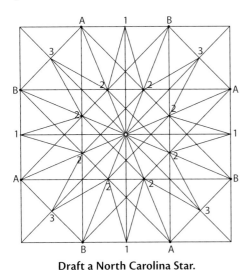

Draft a North Carolina Star.

2. The shaded red point is erased for the North Carolina Star; it remains for this variation.

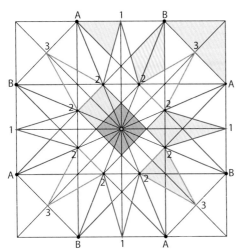

The variation includes the shaded red points.

3. Erase all unnecessary lines, leaving only seamlines.

LeMoyne Star Block

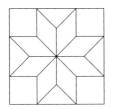

This is the most recognized and basic 8-pointed star design. From this simple structure of a square, triangle, and diamond, many other designs can be developed. By simply fracturing the square, diamond, and triangle, new designs emerge. Up until now, the stars we drafted stood on one point. Going forward, stars will stand on two or four points.

♦♦♦♦♦♦ Noteworthy ♦♦♦♦♦♦

Two same-sized stars, one standing on one point and one standing on two points, have different-sized diamonds.

It is important to notice the relationship among the square, triangle, and diamond: They all share a side. The side of the square, the side of the diamond (a true diamond has four equal sides), and the short sides of the triangle all measure the same, while the long side of the triangle is the diagonal of the square. You will see this relationship over and over in the following block designs.

You will be connecting points, corners, and intersections or creating new intersections to draft further. I will show you how to draft the entire block, even though you only need to go far enough to identify the needed shapes. As the block designs progress from simple and few pieces to more complex and many pieces, the process remains the same—one step at a time, done carefully and accurately. I just love sharing this information with you; let's get started.

TO DRAFT A 6″ (FINISHED) BLOCK:

1. Draft a 6″ Basic Underlying Structure (page 45).

2. Working from the top and going clockwise, use a **red** pencil to connect each A to the opposite B and to the second B.

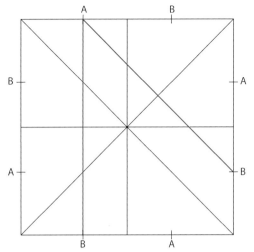

Draft the Basic Underlying Structure and connect A's to B's.

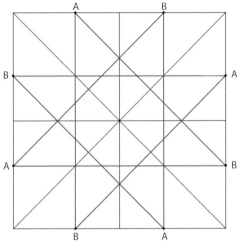

All A's and B's connected in red

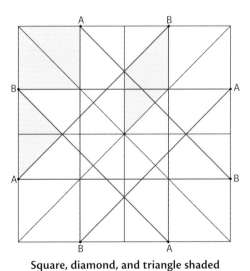

Square, diamond, and triangle shaded

3. Erase all unnecessary lines, leaving only seamlines.

Morning Star Block

The Morning Star block is simply a LeMoyne Star with each diamond fractured into four diamonds by finding and connecting the midpoint of each side of each diamond. Refer to page 23 for information on finding the midpoint of any line.

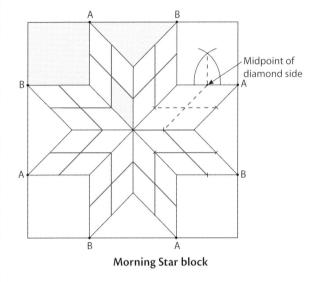

Morning Star block

1. Draft a 6″ LeMoyne Star block (page 54).

2. Refer to page 23 to find the center of each side of the diamond. Then use the compass as a measuring tool to mark all sides of all diamonds. Connect the marks.

Silver and Gold Block

The Silver and Gold block simply divides each diamond in a LeMoyne Star lengthwise from point to point. In my opinion, this block is one of the most beautiful stars; it is also one of the most challenging to sew because it has 16 seams coming together in the center.

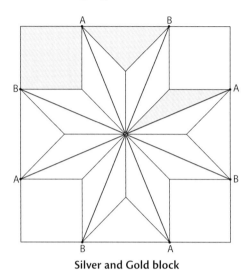

Silver and Gold block

TO DRAFT A 6″ (FINISHED) BLOCK:

1. Draft a 6″ LeMoyne star block (page 54).

2. Connect A to A opposite each other and B to B opposite each other through the center.

Cornucopia Block

This block begins as a LeMoyne Star but with the two diamonds removed and a handle added.

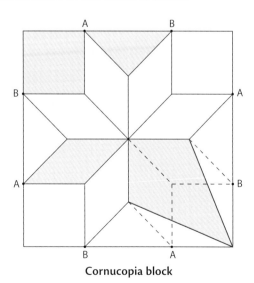

Cornucopia block

TO DRAFT A 6″ (FINISHED) BLOCK:

1. Draft a 6″ LeMoyne Star (page 54).

2. Erase 2 adjoining diamonds and a corner square. Connect 2 diamonds to the corner.

St. Louis Star Block

Connecting A's and B's to each other completely changes the LeMoyne Star block.

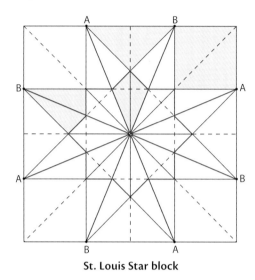

St. Louis Star block

TO DRAFT A 6″ (FINISHED) BLOCK:

1. Draft a 6″ LeMoyne Star (page 54); do not erase any lines.

2. Connect A to A opposite each other, through the center, and B to B opposite each other, through the center.

3. Erase the dashed lines.

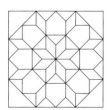

Star of the Magi Block

Drafting of this block results in multiple layers of lines; use colored pencils to help clarify each step. To help minimize the number of lines, carefully look at the block diagram and notice, as you draft, where lines stop in the finished design. You need four shapes: two triangles, one diamond, and one house.

◆◆◆◆◆◆ **Noteworthy** ◆◆◆◆◆◆

To lessen confusion when drafting, after you have drawn a line to connect two points, do not move your ruler until you know where you should place it next.

TO DRAFT A 6˝ (FINISHED) BLOCK:

1. Draft a 6˝ LeMoyne Star (page 54); do not erase any lines.

2. Connect A to B across the corners.

3. Where the horizontal and vertical lines meet the edge, label those 1, 3, 5, and 7.

4. Where the diagonal lines going to the corner intersect with the AB diagonal across the corner, label those 2, 4, 6, and 8.

5. To create 4 of the roof tops, align your ruler edge with points 1 and 3. With a **red** pencil, connect the points, stopping the line when it meets the diamond from each side of the block. Repeat to connect 3 to 5, 5 to 7, and 7 to 1.

6. To create the remaining 4 roof tops, align your ruler edge with 2 and 4. With your **red** pencil again, connect the points, stopping the line when it meets the diamond line. Repeat to connect 4 to 6, 6 to 8, and 8 to 2. You have now revealed the 8 roof tops, corner triangles, and small triangles around the edge of the block.

7. To create the small diamonds, you must first divide the large diamond into 4 diamonds. To do so, you must find the midpoint of each side of each diamond and then connect the midpoints. The midpoint is at the point where the rooftop meets the side of the diamond. Starting at the top edge and working clockwise,

label the midpoints 9–24. Using a light touch with your **blue** pencil, complete the line from number to number. Connect 9 to 16 and 10 to 19. If you look closely, you will see the large diamond is now divided into 4 smaller diamonds. Continue as you connect 11 to 18, 12 to 21, 13 to 20, and 14 to 23. Then connect 15 to 22 and 17 to 24. This process reveals the smaller diamond and the sides of the house.

8. With your orange pencil, connect the lower tips of the 8 small outer diamonds to create the octagon. At this point, all 4 shapes are revealed.

9. If you look closely at the block diagram and your drafting, you'll see that when you divided the diamonds, as the lines traveled through the octagon, 8 more diamonds and 8 triangles formed the small center star.

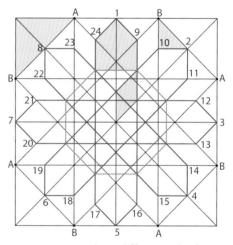

Draft a LeMoyne Star, using a different color for each step.

10. Erase all unnecessary lines, leaving only seamlines.

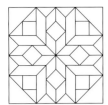

Dutch Rose Block

This block is pieced from five shapes: two triangles, one diamond, one square, and one parallelogram.

TO DRAFT A 6″ (FINISHED) BLOCK:

1. Draft a 6″ LeMoyne Star (page 54); do not erase any lines. Connect A to B across the corners.

2. Where the horizontal and vertical lines meet the block edge, label those 1, 3, 5, and 7.

3. Where the diagonal line going toward the corner intersects with the AB diagonal across the corner, label those intersections 2, 4, 6, and 8.

4. Align your ruler edge with 1 and 3. To minimize lines, look at the block diagram to see where to stop the lines when they meet the diamond edge from both sides of the block. Use your **red** pencil to connect 1 to 3. Continue almost connecting 3 to 5, 5 to 7, and 7 to 1. This creates the small triangles at the edge and one side of two diamonds.

5. Align your ruler edge with 2 and 4. Use your **red** pencil to connect the points, stopping the line at the diamond edge. Repeat for 4 to 6, 6 to 8, and 8 to 2. This creates the 4 small corner squares.

6. To create the 4 squares on-point (these are the same size as the corner squares), align your ruler edge with 2 and 4 again. Mark dots where the ruler edge intersects the 3-7 line. Repeat for 4 to 6 (the 5-1 line), 6 to 8 (the 7-3 line), and 8 to 2 (the 1-5 line). With your **blue** pencil, lightly connect the marks to create a larger single square on-point. This creates the 2 outside edges of the 4 small on-point squares.

7. To complete the remaining 2 edges of the 4 squares and one edge of the center diamonds, align your ruler edge diagonally with 2 corners of the small red squares. With your **blue** pencil, draw a line from the large on-point square to the vertical 1-5 line. Draw a similar line from the large on-point square to the horizontal 7-3 line; make 4.

8. To create the parallelogram, align your ruler with the corners of 2 opposite on-point squares. With your **orange** pencil, draw a line from the triangle point to the diagonal line, running from corner to corner from both edges. Repeat 4 times to make 8 parallelograms.

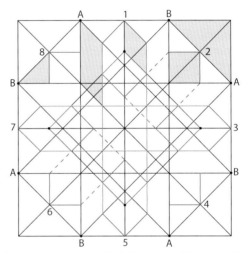

Draft a LeMoyne Star. Label the vertical, horizontal, and diagonal lines. Use different colors to connect the points.

9. Erase all unnecessary lines, leaving only seamlines.

DRAFTING FOR THE CREATIVE QUILTER

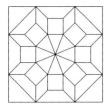

Castle Wall Block

You will need five shapes to piece this block: a square, triangle, diamond, trapezoid, and pie-shaped wedge.

TO DRAFT A 6″ (FINISHED) BLOCK:

1. Draft a 6″ LeMoyne Star (page 54); do not erase any lines.

2. Connect A to B across the 4 corners.

3. Label the intersections inside each diamond 1–8.

4. To create the center octagon, use your **red** pencil to connect 1 to 2 to 3 to 4 to 5 to 6 to 7 to 8 to 1.

5. Use those same intersections to create the pie-shaped wedges. With your **red** pencil, connect 1 to 5, 2 to 6, 3 to 7, and 4 to 8.

6. To create the 8 small diamonds, you must determine the midpoint between the outer tips of the diamonds positioned at the A and B points around the edge of the square and the opposite tip, which corresponds to the 8 corners of the octagon. To do that, work clockwise from the top to connect each A to the next A and each B to the next B. This creates 16 new intersections, each denoted by a dot.

7. To create 2 sides of the 8 squares and the 2 remaining sides of the 8 diamonds, use your **blue** pencil to connect each octagon corner (1–8) to 2 intersections.

8. With your orange pencil, connect 2 dots to create the 8 squares and to reveal the last shape, the trapezoid.

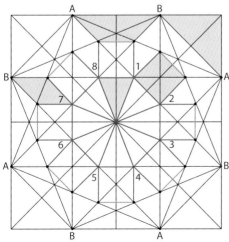

Draft a LeMoyne Star. Connect A's and B's. Label and connect the intersections. Use different colors for Steps 4–8.

9. Erase all unnecessary lines, leaving only seamlines.

DRAFTING USING A HANDHELD CALCULATOR

Although you can draft 8-pointed star designs using graph paper, pencil, compass, and rulers, as described on pages 44–59, you can also draft a variety of 8-pointed star designs using a calculator. When drafting these designs with graph paper and pencil, you choose the size of the block and then draft the design within that space to determine the size shapes needed to sew the block. When drafting using a calculator, however, you still make the same choices of block design and block size, but rather than draft the entire block, you calculate the size of the shapes needed and then draw those shapes on either 8- or 10-to-the-inch graph paper. Seam allowances (¼″) are then added to all sides of each shape. When using a calculator, the results will be in decimals. Refer to the Decimal Equivalent Chart (page 68) to convert decimals to fractions.

To illustrate the basics, let's start with the most elementary 8-pointed star, the LeMoyne Star block. It is drafted from eight equal 45° divisions of a circle (pie-shaped wedges), radiating out from the center (360° ÷ 8 = 45°), not on a grid of equal divisions across and down the block as described in the grid-based drafting category (see pages 10–11). The divisions that fit along the outside edge of the LeMoyne Star block are not equal, but the distance between the star points is equal.

The three shapes that create the LeMoyne Star block are a square, a 45° diamond (a true diamond has four equal sides), and a triangle (which is the diagonal half of the square). By looking at the block, you can see that these three shapes have a relationship—the side of the square, the side of the diamond, and the two short sides of the triangle are the exact same size. Therefore, if you know the size of the square, you know the size of the diamond and triangle.

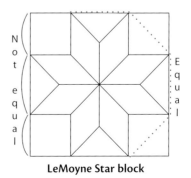

LeMoyne Star block

Even though the LeMoyne Star block is based on eight equal divisions of a circle, rather than on equal divisions along the edge of a square, the divisions along the edge of the LeMoyne Star block still have a relationship. This relationship is based on a streamlined understanding of the mathematical theory of the Pythagorean theorem: $a^2 + b^2 = c^2$. This theorem states that the diagonal of a square (or the long side of a right-angle triangle) is always 1.414 times longer than the finished size of the side of the square or right-angle triangle. This is *always* the case, without fail. Remember, I have no formal math education, so if I can do this, you can too! It is not as important to remember the theorem as it is to understand the relationship between the side of a square and its diagonal or between the side of a right-angle triangle and its diagonal.

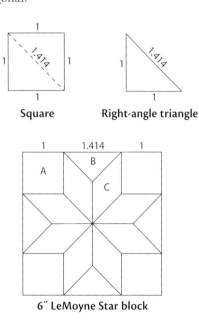

Square   **Right-angle triangle**

6″ LeMoyne Star block

Looking at the top edge of the block diagram, notice how the theorem applies to the LeMoyne Star block. Assign the 1 value to the two squares and the 1.414 value to the middle division of the block (which is the diagonal of the square). When you add the three values together (1 + 1.414 + 1), the sum of the parts is 3.414. If you divide the size of the block you desire (6″) by the sum of the parts (6″ ÷ 3.414 = 1.7574 = 1¾″), the result is the finished size of the square, which is also the size of all four sides of the diamond and the two short sides of the triangle (remember, the triangle is the diagonal half of the square). When you know the shapes and their sizes, draw those shapes on 8-to-the-inch graph paper (in this case) and add seam allowances to all sides of each shape. Then rotary cut or make templates to cut

your fabric, depending on whether the sizes are ruler friendly.

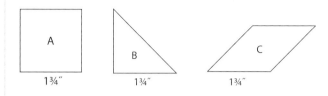

This method also allows you to *choose* the size of the corner square for the LeMoyne Star, which tells you the size of the diamond and the triangle. You might do this if you were making a repeat block quilt and you wanted to work with a size with which you are comfortable or that is ruler friendly. It is only important that they are all the same size. Let's say you are making a medallion-style quilt, and the size of the block isn't as important as the size of the pieces you want to work with. If you choose the size of the corner square and multiply that by 3.414 (the sum of the parts), the result is the block size. For example, if you choose to work with a 1¾″ corner square, 1.7574 (always use the decimal) × 3.414 = 5.9997, which is the decimal equivalent of 6″, which would be the block size.

In summary, to determine the size of the square, diamond, and triangle for a 6″ LeMoyne Star block, divide the block size by the sum of the parts, which is 3.414. To determine the block size for a LeMoyne Star, multiply the sum of the parts (3.414) by the desired size of the corner square.

This theorem applies to many other 8-pointed star blocks. Although the sum of the parts can change, depending on the complexity of the block, the principle and formula remain the same.

I use this method when appropriate. With it I do not need to draft the entire block to identify my shapes or see how they are situated to each other. I have a line drawing or a photo or a quilt to show me how the block looks and how the shapes are situated to each other; I just need to know what size the shapes are for any block size I choose.

Now that you have a clear understanding of the LeMoyne Star block, I want to show you how this same principle is applied to other 8-pointed star designs, including some that we drafted on graph paper earlier. Carefully look at each design and notice the relationship among the squares, triangles, and diamonds. This process will become logical and sensible. Take your time.

DRAFTING FOR THE CREATIVE QUILTER

Star of Many Points Block

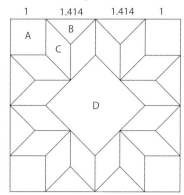

6″ Star of Many Points block

Sum of parts: 4.828

1. 6″ ÷ 4.828 (sum of parts) = 1.2428 = 1¼″, which is the size of the A square, B triangle, and C diamond.

2. To find the size of the D square, notice that the side of the D square is the same as the distance across the side of the two C diamonds; therefore the square is 2½″ (1¼″ twice).

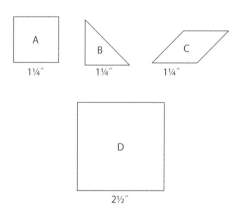

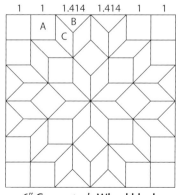

Carpenter's Wheel Block

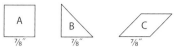

6″ Carpenter's Wheel block

Sum of parts: 6.828

1. 6″ ÷ 6.828 (sum of parts) = 0.8787 = ⅞″, which is the size of the A square, B triangle, and C diamond.

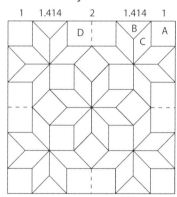

◆◆◆◆◆◆ **Noteworthy** ◆◆◆◆◆◆

A Carpenter's Wheel block is always twice the size of the small star at its center, and the size of the star in the center is always half the size of the block. The Carpenter's Wheel block is the basic structure I used to design *Sedona* (page 116).

Snow Crystals Block

6″ Snow Crystals block

Sum of parts: 6.828

1. 6″ ÷ 6.828 (sum of parts) = 0.8787 = ⅞″, which is the size of the A square, B triangle, and C diamond.

2. As for the size of the D rectangle, the short side is ⅞″ and the long side is 1¾″.

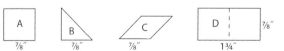

Flying Swallows Block

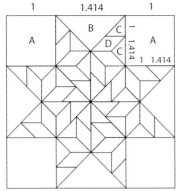

6″ Flying Swallows block

Sum of parts: 3.414

1. 6″ ÷ 3.414 (sum of parts) = 1.7574 = 1¾″, which is the size of the A square and B triangle.

2. To find the size of the smaller C triangle and D diamond situated along one edge of the A square, you first need to determine the sum of the parts along that edge. There are two C triangles along one edge; these two triangles are the same, although they each have a different side touching the square. Therefore, the assigned value is 1 for the short side and 1.414 for the long side, and the sum of the parts is 2.414. If you divide the size of the square (1.7574) by the sum of the parts (2.414), the result is the size of the C triangle on its short sides and the size of all 4 sides of the D diamond.

1.7574 ÷ 2.414 = 0.7280 = $^7/_{10}$″

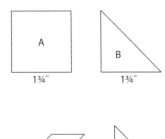

In this case, the A square and B triangle would be drawn on 8-to-the-inch graph paper, whereas shapes C and D would be drawn on 10-to-the-inch graph paper.

Rolling Star Block

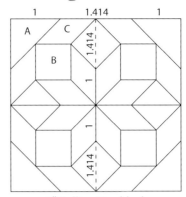

6″ Rolling Star block

1. To determine the size of the A corner triangle, divide the block size by the sum of the parts along the edge.

Sum of parts: 3.414

2. 6″ ÷ 3.414 (sum of parts) = 1.7574 = 1¾″, which is the size of the A triangle.

3. To determine the size of the B square and C diamond, you need to determine the sum of the parts inside the block.

Sum of parts: 4.828

4. 6″ ÷ 4.828 (sum of parts) = 1.2427 = 1¼″ for the B square and C diamond.

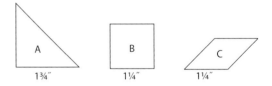

Dutch Rose Block

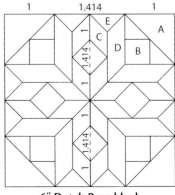

6″ Dutch Rose block

To determine the size of the A triangles, divide the block size by the sum of the parts along the edge.

DRAFTING FOR THE CREATIVE QUILTER

Sum of parts: 3.414

1. 6″ ÷ 3.414 (sum of parts) = 1.7574 = 1¾″, which is the size of the A triangles.

2. To determine the size of the B square, C diamond, D parallelogram, and E triangle, you need to determine the sum of the parts inside the block.

Sum of parts: 6.828

3. 6″ ÷ 6.828 (sum of parts) = 0.8787 = ⅞″ which is the size of the B square, C diamond, and E triangle.

The D parallelogram is ⅞″ on its 2 short sides and 1¾″ on its 2 long sides.

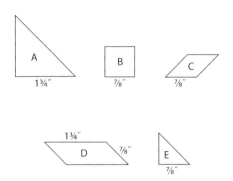

North Carolina Lily Block

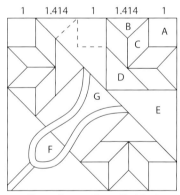

6″ North Carolina Lily block

Sum of parts: 5.828

1. 6″ ÷ 5.828 (sum of parts) = 1.0295″ = 1″, which is the size of the A square, B triangle (short sides), and C diamond.

2. The size of the short side of the D triangle is the diagonal measurement of the A square (1″ × 1.414 = 1.414″ = 1⁴⁄₁₀″).

3. The size of the short side of the E triangle is the diagonal measurement of the A square plus the short side of the A square (1.414″ + 1″ = 2.414″ = 2⁴⁄₁₀″).

4. The size of the short side of the F triangle is the measurement of the A square twice plus its diagonal measurement (1″ + 1″ + 1.414″ = 3.414″ = 3⁴⁄₁₀″).

5. The two short sides of the G rectangle are the measurement of the A square twice (1″ + 1″ = 2″).

6. The two longer sides of the G rectangle are the diagonal measurement of the A square plus the short side of the A square (1.414″ + 1″ = 2.414″ = 2⁴⁄₁₀″).

All shapes should be drawn on 10-to-the-inch graph paper.

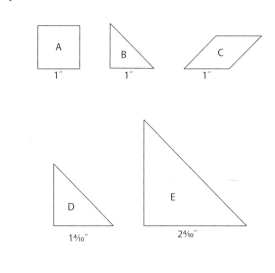

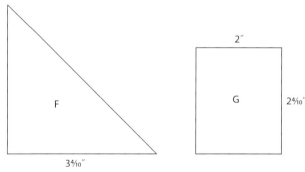

Wheel of Fortune Block

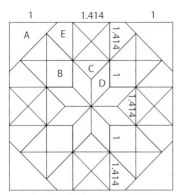

6″ Wheel of Fortune block

1. To determine the size of the A triangle, divide the block size by the sum of the parts along the edge (3.414).

Sum of parts: 3.414

6″ ÷ 3.414 (sum of parts) = 1.7574 = 1¾″, which is the size of the A triangle.

2. To determine the size of the remaining shapes (the B square, C triangle, D diamond, and E kite), you need to determine the sum of the parts inside the block (6.242).

6″ ÷ 6.242 = 0.9612 = 1″, which is the size of the B square, C triangle, and D diamond.

3. The E kite shape's long sides are the diagonal measurement of the B square (0.9612″ × 1.414 = 1.3591″ = 1⅜″). Draw 2 lines each 1⅜″ at 45° to each other.

4. To determine the short sides of the E kite, draw a line at a 90° angle from each end of the long sides of the E kite until they intersect.

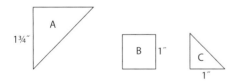

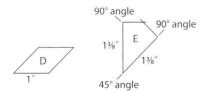

Star of the Magi Block

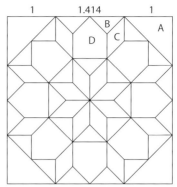

6″ Star of the Magi block

To determine the size of the A triangle, divide the block size by the sum of the parts (3.414).

Sum of parts: 3.414

6″ ÷ 3.414 (sum of parts) = 1.7574 = 1¾″, which is the size of the short side of the A triangle.

To determine the size of the B triangle, C diamond, and D house, carefully examine the block diagram as you follow Steps 1–4 below.

1. To determine the size of the B triangle and C diamond, you first need to find the measurement of the middle division of the block (the distance between the 2 diamond points), which is the diagonal measurement of the A triangle: 1.7574″ × 1.414 = 2.4849″ = 2½″. If you divide that in half, you end up with the measurement of the long side of the B triangle: 2.4849″ ÷ 2 = 1.2424″ = 1¼″.

2. To determine the size of the short side of the B triangle, divide 1.2424″ (long side of B) by 1.414 to get 0.8786″, or ⅞″.

3. Because the short side of the B triangle fits to the C diamond, it is also ⅞″.

4. Look at the D house shape. The top 2 edges of the roof are the same as the short side of the B triangle, or ⅞″; the 2 sides of the D house shape are the same as the side of the C diamond (which is also the same as the roof top edges), or ⅞″. The bottom of the D house shape is the same as the long side of the B triangle, or 1¼″.

5. The diamond and the triangle that create the small star are shapes B and C.

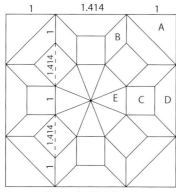

draw a line to connect the 2 ends of the 1″ line to the mark to create the E wedge shape.

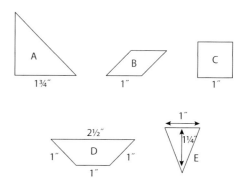

Castle Wall Block

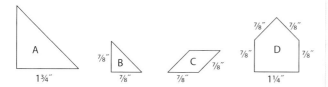

6″ Castle Wall block

For this design, you will calculate two different sums of parts. Find the sum of parts along the edge of the block.

Sum of parts: 3.414

1. 6″ ÷ 3.414 (sum of parts) = 1.7574 = 1¾″ for the A triangles.

2. To find the measurement of the remaining shapes (B, C, D, E), add up the sum of the parts inside the block: 1 + 1.414 + 1 + 1.414 + 1 = 5.828.

Sum of parts: 5.828

3. 6″ ÷ 5.828 (sum of parts) = 1.0295″ = 1″ for the B diamond and C square.

4. The long side of the D trapezoid is the diagonal measurement of the A triangle (1.7574″ × 1.414 = 2.484 = 2½″). The 3 remaining sides of the D trapezoid are the same as the B and C shapes, or 1″.

5. To determine the size of the E wedge shape, you first need to know the size of the octagon in the center of the block. The octagon is the diagonal measure of the A triangle (1.7574″ × 1.414 = 2.484″ = 2½″). The short side of the E wedge is 1″. Find the center of the 1″ short side of the E wedge (½″) and measure down half the size of the octagon. Then make a mark (half of 2½″ is 1¼″) and

Radiant Feathered Star Block

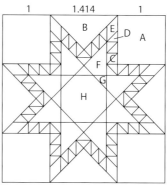

15″ Radiant Feathered Star block

DRAFTING METHOD 1

This first method is based on choosing the size of the feather first. This is my preferred method because there are more feathers than any other shape, so I want them to be a ruler-friendly number for cutting.

1. Decide the size of the feather. In this example, we will use 1″. Draw the C and D feathers on 8-to-the-inch graph paper.

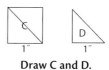

Draw C and D.

2. Referring to the drawing of the Radiant Feathered Star above, decide how many feathers you want to fit along the side of the F kite. Here, we will use 3, although you could choose as many as you like.

3. On 8-to-the-inch graph paper, draw a line 3″ and draw another line 3″ at a 45° angle to the first.

4. The 2 short sides of the F kite are developed by drawing a line at a 90° angle from both 3″ lines until they intersect.

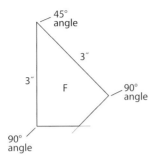

5. To determine the size of the E diamond, multiply the short side of the D feather (1″) by 1.414.

$$1″ \times 1.414 = 1^4/_{10}″$$

6. On 10-to-the-inch graph paper, draw the E diamond so all 4 sides measure $1^4/_{10}″$ at 45° angles to each other.

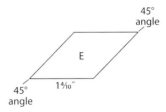

Draw E.

7. To determine the size of the A square, add up the inches that fit along the side of the A square.

$$1″ + 1″ + 1″ + 1.414″ = 4.414″ = 4^4/_{10}″$$

8. On 10-to-the-inch graph paper, draw the A square.

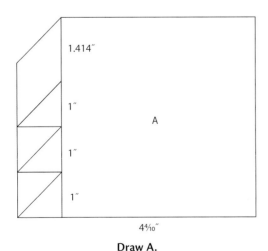

Draw A.

9. The B triangle is the diagonal half of the A square. On 10-to-the-inch graph paper, draw the B triangle.

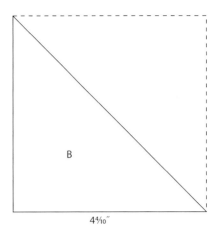

Draw B.

10. To determine the size of the G triangle, measure the short side of the F kite; it should be 1¼″.

11. On 8-to-the-inch graph paper, draw a triangle with short sides that measure 1¼″ and connect their ends.

Draw G.

12. To determine the size of the H octagon, add the short side of the G triangle twice, plus its diagonal measurement once.

$$1.25″ \times 1.414 = 1.7675″ \text{ (diagonal measurement of G triangle)}$$

$$1.25″ + 1.25″ + 1.7675″ = 4.2675″ = 4¼″$$

13. On 8-to-the-inch graph paper, draw a 4¼″ square. Come 1¼″ (the size of the short sides of the G triangle) in from each side of each corner. Connect the points and erase the triangles to reveal the H octagon shape.

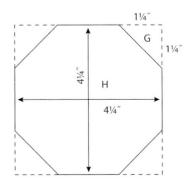

Draw a square, and then draw diagonal corner lines.

DRAFTING METHOD 2

This method uses a calculator and is based on choosing the size of the block first.

1. To determine the size of the A square and B triangle, divide the size of the block (15") by the sum of the parts (3.414).

$$15" \div 3.414 = 4.3936" = 4.4" = 4^4/_{10}"$$

2. On 10-to-the-inch graph paper, draw a $4^4/_{10}"$ A square and B triangle.

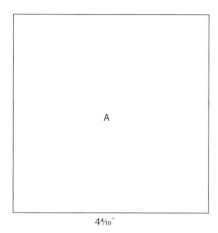

$4^4/_{10}"$

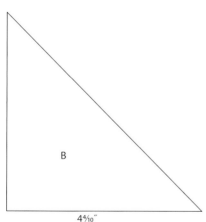

$4^4/_{10}"$

Draw A and B.

3. To determine the size of the C and D feathers, add the 1 values and 1.414 values that fit along the side of the A square and divide that into the actual size of the corner square (4.3936). There are 3 triangles with a 1 value and 1 diamond with a 1.414 value, because the side of the E diamond is equal to the long side of the half-square triangle, which is always 1.414 times longer than its side.

$$4.3936" \div 4.414 = 0.9953" = 1" \text{ C and D feathers}$$

4. To determine the size of the E diamond, multiply the size of the feather by 1.414.

$$0.9953" \times 1.414 = 1.4073" = 1^4/_{10}" \text{ E diamond}$$

5. On 10-to-the-inch graph paper, draw a 45° diamond, with all sides $1^4/_{10}"$.

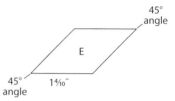

Draw E.

6. To determine the size of the H octagon, you first need to determine the size of the center square. To do that, add the size of the 2 corner squares to the 2 tracks of feathers. Subtract that answer from the finished size of the block.

$$4.3936" + 4.3936" + 0.9953" + 0.9953" = 10.7778"$$

$$15" - 10.7778" = 4.2222" = 4\frac{1}{4}" \text{ center square}$$

7. Divide 4.222" by 3.414 to find the size of the G corner triangles of the H octagon.

$$4.222" \div 3.414 = 1.2367" = 1\frac{1}{4}" \text{ G corner triangles}$$

8. On 8-to-the-inch graph paper, draw a $4\frac{1}{4}"$ square. Then, measure in from each corner in both directions $1\frac{1}{4}"$. Connect the marks diagonally and erase the corners.

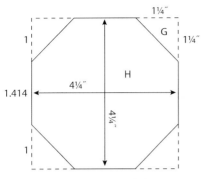

Draw a square, and then draw diagonal corner lines.

9. Shape F is the kite shape. The long sides are equal to 3 feathers, or 3″. The short sides of the F kite are the same as the short sides of the G corner triangles, or 1¼″. On 8-to-the-inch graph paper, draw 2 lines 3″ long at 45° angles from each other. The short sides of the F kite are each 1¼″ long at 90° angles to each 3″ line.

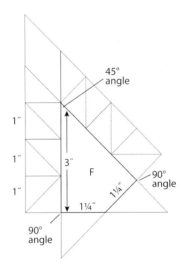

Draw F.

DECIMAL EQUIVALENT CHART

When working on a calculator, answers are given in decimals rather than fractions—decimals are calculator numbers, while fractions are ruler numbers. During the calculation process of each drafting step, work with decimals until all the calculating for that step is complete. Then refer to the Decimal Equivalent Chart and convert your answer to a fraction. If the answer on the calculator screen is not in this chart, find the two numbers it falls between and subtract to find the difference from both. Use the decimal equivalent that is the closest to your number. The difference between the numbers listed in the chart is ¹⁄₃₂″. If your number were to fall in between two numbers, the difference would be ¹⁄₆₄″. This is an

acceptable tolerance for patchwork. There may also be times when the number on the calculator would be most accurate if it were to remain in tenths; in that case, you would use 10-to-the-inch graph paper to draw your shapes. Decimal equivalents matter; use your good sense to determine your equivalents.

Decimal	Fraction
0.0313	¹⁄₃₂
0.0625	²⁄₃₂ (¹⁄₁₆)
0.0938	³⁄₃₂
0.1250	⁴⁄₃₂ (¹⁄₈)
0.1563	⁵⁄₃₂
0.1875	⁶⁄₃₂ (³⁄₁₆)
0.2188	⁷⁄₃₂
0.2500	⁸⁄₃₂ (¹⁄₄)
0.2813	⁹⁄₃₂
0.3125	¹⁰⁄₃₂ (⁵⁄₁₆)
0.3438	¹¹⁄₃₂
0.3750	¹²⁄₃₂ (³⁄₈)
0.4063	¹³⁄₃₂
0.4375	¹⁴⁄₃₂ (⁷⁄₁₆)
0.4688	¹⁵⁄₃₂
0.5000	¹⁶⁄₃₂ (¹⁄₂)
0.5313	¹⁷⁄₃₂
0.5625	¹⁸⁄₃₂ (⁹⁄₁₆)
0.5938	¹⁹⁄₃₂
0.6250	²⁰⁄₃₂ (⁵⁄₈)
0.6563	²¹⁄₃₂
0.6875	²²⁄₃₂ (¹¹⁄₁₆)
0.7188	²³⁄₃₂
0.7500	²⁴⁄₃₂ (³⁄₄)
0.7813	²⁵⁄₃₂
0.8125	²⁶⁄₃₂ (¹³⁄₁₆)
0.8438	²⁷⁄₃₂
0.8750	²⁸⁄₃₂ (⁷⁄₈)
0.9063	²⁹⁄₃₂
0.9375	³⁰⁄₃₂ (¹⁵⁄₁₆)
0.9688	³¹⁄₃₂
1.0000	³²⁄₃₂ (1)

DRAFTING FOR THE CREATIVE QUILTER

Design

Design

Design is the arrangement of details that make up a work of art.

I have no formal education or credentials in design; therefore, I will simply share with you my approach to design when making quilts. First and foremost, my goal is always to make beautiful quilts, while also being challenged creatively and technically. I am a traditional quiltmaker at heart, and my focus, when I began making quilts more than 30 years ago, was workmanship—how to cut and sew quilts together accurately. Color and design were not subjects I consciously knew anything about, nor did they particularly interest me. Over time, however, as my technical skills improved, my interest in design and color heightened. I wanted to make my own quilts rather than work from an existing pattern. I wanted to change sizes and settings, add details, and mix different scales.

As a new quilter, armed with a pattern and fabric, I wanted to cut and sew as quickly as possible—no planning for me; just forge ahead. The results of those early efforts gleaned less-than-satisfactory quilts. From those experiences, I can tell you that it's not fun to complete a block or quilt and then, upon closer evaluation and reflection, discover areas that could have and/or should have been corrected or improved if I hadn't been in such a hurry to finish. After spending such a significant amount of time making a quilt, I want to love it, be excited by the results, and be satisfied with my efforts, not disappointed.

I often, but not always, design my quilts in one of two ways—either on an overall grid or using existing blocks and then fracturing the space within their shapes to create new designs. Rough-cut mock-ups in actual size, mirrors, sketches, scale drawings, a design wall, and a camera all contribute to a design plan, while still allowing serendipity to occur. I have learned that taking the time to create a design plan is a fun, exciting, creative, educational process, and I love my quilts when they are finished because I have composed them piece by piece, according to my design plans.

Once I have a design plan, I create a color plan by making a mock-up of either one-quarter or one-eighth of a design for symmetrical designs, by mocking up the complete design for asymmetrical designs, or by working on the design wall and composing each piece by folding and interviewing each fabric when working on an overall grid. The mock-up process allows me to compose every color and fabric in my quilt by placing mirrors around the mock-up to see the complete design. If I do not create a design and color plan, I'm essentially guessing at color, fabric, and design choices and hoping it all works out.

There are three disciplines in quiltmaking: color, design, and workmanship. Three separate areas; three different processes. When I make quilts, I separate color and design from workmanship, because I do not want my creativity to be influenced or intimidated by my technical skill level. My attitude is that I will get it sewn somehow. Design and color are freer, more playful, and more creative; whereas workmanship is more focused, deliberate, and orchestrated.

Perhaps you've gone to quilt shows or looked at quilts in books or magazines and known intuitively whether or not a quilt is successful, even though you might not be able to identify why. Specific visual design elements help guide creative visual design, and when those elements are not used in harmony, the design can falter.

Color is what gets all the attention and applause. It gives quilts their personality and defines our personal style. Color can determine the character of a quilt—whether the quilt is bold, dynamic, soft, rich, whimsical, serene, and so on. At the end of the day, it's your quilt; so, if you are pleased with the results, that is all that matters.

Value is the amount of light or dark in a color. Value placement, which is what actually creates design, is the most important principle. How and where we place the light, medium, and dark values in our quilts creates the design and enables the viewer to decipher and read that design. How large or small the value difference is between two values that touch is called *contrast*. As you examine your quilt when designing, consider the value. Does it seem to all mush together? Perhaps you need more exaggerated value contrast in some areas to clarify the design. Does it seem choppy and sharp rather than smooth? Perhaps creating subtler or lower contrast in some areas will solve that problem. It is always helpful to look at your quilt from a distance. Use a reducing glass, look at a photo of the quilt, or get at least 20 feet from it. You want to be as excited about it from a distance as you are right up close to it.

Texture can be created through the quilting stitches, the fabric type (silk, cotton, flannel), the size and style of the print on the fabric (stripes, plaids, florals, dots), embellishments (buttons, embroidery, beads, paint, foil), or any combination of these elements.

Shape or Form is anything that has width and length, such as circles, triangles, squares, rectangles, leaves, flowers, and so on.

Lines in quilts can be curved, straight, jagged, or a combination of these.

Scale is the size of one shape relative to another. Different sizes of shapes in quilts create detail and interest.

Direction is how the design moves or draws the eye vertically, horizontally, or diagonally. Many of my quilts are symmetrical, medallion-style quilts and have a radial direction, advancing outward from the center.

Think of these design elements as ingredients in a recipe. Each has its own purpose, taste, and property. In a recipe, if one ingredient is used too much or if you leave an ingredient out, the whole recipe is at risk and can fail. This is true in design as well. If the design employs all the elements in a balanced way, the quilt will be visually successful.

Successful quilt designs are achieved by mixing and blending the design elements to create harmony, unity, balance, and variety. Unity holds a quilt design together. Our quilts need some visual organization or relationship between the elements. When unity is lacking, quilts can seem disconnected, confusing, and chaotic. Unity is accomplished through repetition of design elements, because repeating a particular design element gives a sense of order. However, you must also be careful not to overdo it and create monotony. Variety, which enhances design as well as creates interest for the viewer, is achieved by changing fabric prints, color value, and scale. Both unity and variety are necessary for successful design. When one is not present, the design will suffer.

These are some simple, basic guidelines for creating successful designs. In the end, reading, taking color and design classes, practicing, and experience are always the best teachers. However, remember that there are always exceptions to every rule; so learn to follow and trust your heart and make quilts you love.

Designing on an Overall Grid

A grid is a formation of equal-sized shapes, such as squares, rectangles, triangles, diamonds, and so forth. The total design area of the quilt can be square or rectangular. My preference and experience at this time is to work on a grid formation of squares.

Square formation

Vertical rectangular formation

Horizontal rectangular formation

My initial experience designing on a grid was in the early 1990s. It was a quilt titled *Always* that I designed for my husband for Valentine's Day. I assigned a grid value of 1″ for the background and doubled that (2″) for the hearts—simple and effective.

Always, 32″ × 34″, designed, pieced, and quilted by the author.

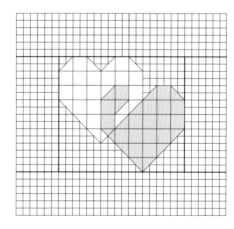

Always drawing

Since that time, I have drawn numerous quilts designed on an overall grid. Some have become quilts, and some have not. A few of those drawings follow, with a photograph where applicable. Borders are not included on the drawings.

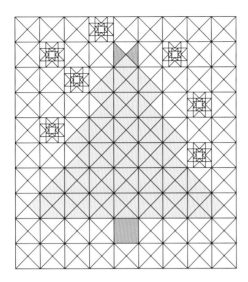

O' Christmas Tree drawing, 1½″ grid value and 2 × 2 grid space (3″ square), which I divided into quarters diagonally to create an allover grid of quarter-square triangles to develop the design.

O' Christmas Tree, 35″ × 38″, designed, pieced, and quilted by the author.

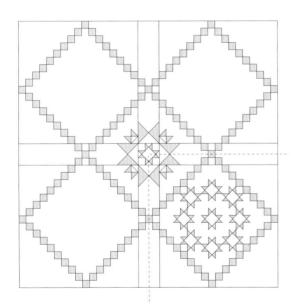

Circle of Stars IV drawing, ½″ grid value (Dashed line indicates mirror placement.)

Circle of Stars IV, 25″ × 25″, designed, pieced, and quilted by the author.

DRAFTING FOR THE CREATIVE QUILTER

Pinwheel Quilt drawing, 1½″ grid value
(Darkened lines indicate piecing sections.)

Pinwheel Quilt, 27″ × 35″, designed, pieced, and quilted
by the author.

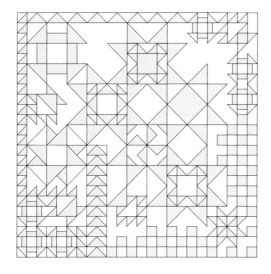

Drawing of Star, Basket, and Churn Dash blocks
with filler shapes (sawtooth, checkerboard, dogtooth)

Drawing of stars in different sizes—My intention was to
assign a 1½″ grid value. (x indicates placement of a 1½″ star.)

Working within a grid format allows me to design my own quilts in a familiar environment of simple squares. Working within a grid format is structured, safe, organized, and orderly. You make all the choices. You decide space composition, size of the grid, and size of the shapes. The grid size determines quilt size. For example, if you assign a grid value of 2″ and your design covers a 20 × 30 grid space, your quilt size will be 40″ × 60″.

Even though you are working on an underlying grid of equal-sized squares, the composition of your quilt design can include different shapes and sizes based on multiples of the individual grid size. For example, if you are working on a 2″ grid of squares, you can include 4″ squares, triangles, and so forth.

You could also include any size shape you want in your quilt and then fill in the difference to put yourself back in sync with the grid. This happened to me in *Sampler Supreme*, which was developed on a 1½″ grid. The 3-Dimensional Cube block measures 6″ × 7″ finished. Six is divisible by 1½″ (4 grids), but seven is not equally divisible by the 1½″ grid size. The next higher number that is divisible by 1½″ is 7½″ (5 grids), so I simply added a ½″ strip to the bottom of the block to put myself back on track and in sync with the grid size. The 3-Dimensional Cube block took up the space of 4 × 5 grids.

When choosing the initial grid value, take into consideration visual balance. You can always change the grid value if your first choice isn't working.

If you do not have a specific idea for creating a quilt, the following questions might help nudge your creativity and give you ideas.

- Do you want to follow a certain theme, such as a specific holiday, spiritual theme, or friendship?

- Do you want to explore a favorite block or work with a favorite block in different sizes?

- Do you want to express a feeling or emotion, such as joy, love, happiness, or patriotism?

- Is there a color or combination of colors you've always wanted to use?

- Do you have a fabric that inspires you?

- Do you want to honor or celebrate an occasion or relationship?

Once you have an idea, acknowledge what you know about that idea and what you want to include in your design. Design freely without getting involved in color, fabric, or how it will get sewn. Only think about design—the arrangement of details that make up a work of art.

Remember, whenever you draft, design, calculate, or figure out anything in patchwork, seam allowance is never included.

DESIGN PROCESS FOR SAMPLER SUPREME

Sampler Supreme, 44½″ × 47½″, designed and pieced by author, machine quilted by Lois Russell of San Diego, CA.

I knew that I wanted to make a sampler that incorporates a variety of block designs based on a variety of drafting categories in a variety of sizes that offers a variety of skill challenges. I wanted to arrange the blocks on an overall grid format to give the quilt a more contemporary feel. I chose a 1½″ grid value.

Next, I decided specifics. I chose to include eight different blocks—three major in size and five minor in size. Chrysanthemum (Spiraling Squares) would be the largest (15″), then Trip Around the World (10½″) and Interlocking Squares (12″), and finally Corn and Beans, Sawtooth Star Variation, Ten-Pointed Star, Hexagon, and one block from the Fan drafting category would all be 6″. These were my initial decisions; change can occur at anytime . . . and often does.

Next I went with ¼″ graph paper. With a grid value of 1½″, I drew the outside perimeter of my quilt, without borders. I started with 31 × 31 grids. Within that space, I sketched a rough composition of the placement of each block on the grid. For example, if a block finished 12″ and my grid value was 1½″, 12″ ÷ 1.5″ = 8, that meant that my 12″ block would occupy 8 × 8 grids on my drawing. I did not use a ruler; I just darkened grid lines freehand to put in the space I needed for each block. I did not draw in each block design. Instead, I attempted to create a balanced composition of space based on the block sizes I had already chosen.

#1 indicates placement of the largest block—15″ Chrysanthemum (Spiraling Squares).

#2 indicates placement of the two remaining major blocks—9¾″ Trip Around the World and 12″ Interlocking Squares.

#3 indicates placement of the five remaining 6″ blocks. I tried to keep a sense of balance when arranging them within the gridded space, keeping in mind their relationship to the three major blocks.

#4 indicates multiple-grid areas that could be filled with pieces of beautiful fabric; pieced units, such as half-square triangles, squares-on-point, or appliqué; or a peace symbol.

Nothing is written in stone; this is only the beginning.

Refining the Design

I liked the basic composition and overall feel of the first sketch, but I wanted to make some changes.

- Sampler quilts are all about the blocks, so I wanted to change the area around the blocks (the background area) from all squares to primarily rectangles. The squares seemed a little busy and chaotic, and I thought (just guessing here) that rectangles would be smoother and would enhance the blocks better than squares.

- The first sketch was a 31 × 31 grid. Each grid was 1½″, which meant that my quilt would be 46½″ square without borders. This was too big.

- I felt the background space between the blocks could be less, as it all seemed a little too spread out.

- I also eliminated the #4 multiple-grid filler areas, except for the peace symbol, because I was drifting away from my initial idea of a simple composition.

My second sketch was 27 × 29 grids (40½″ × 43½″), which is smaller than the first. It included less space between the blocks. I also decided to make the 6″ block from the Fan drafting category (page 21) a half-block to add some interest, and I placed it where the #4 rectangular shape had appeared in the upper right area of the first sketch. My sketches are rough; I make notations everywhere, erase, and adjust—a little messy looking, but it works.

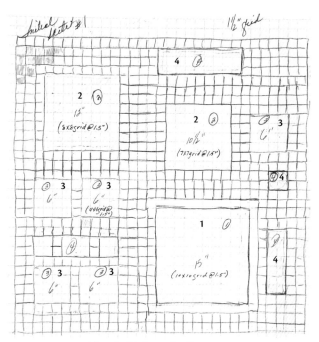

Sketch #1, *Sampler Supreme*

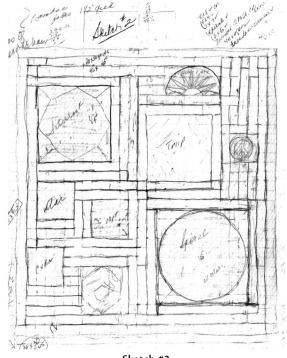

Sketch #2

Translating the Design to Fabric

Then it was time to sew the blocks. My color palette was magenta, blue, teal, and gold. I made a rough-cut mock-up and used mirrors to compose and see each block's color composition before cutting and sewing the fabric. (Refer to the *Sampler Supreme* project instructions on pages 99–115 and Rough-Cut Mock-up and Mirrors on page 91.) I photographed each block's mock-up to show what I did. Only a portion—in most cases one-eighth—of the design needs to be mocked up to see the complete block in the mirrors.

As I sewed the blocks, I made two more changes. I added one more grid of space to the Spiraling Squares block because I wanted to place it inside a circle and then square it. I also discovered when I drafted and sewed the hexagon cube that it was not square but rectangular, which adjusted the number of grids it would occupy from 4 × 4 to 4 × 5 grids.

Composing on the Design Wall

Once I had assembled all the blocks, I moved to the design wall. Based on my second sketch, I roughly sectioned off my design wall by pinning tape measures vertically and horizontally, so I would know the actual size of the total design area. I then divided the design area into quadrants to guide me when positioning the blocks and the filler rectangles. If you do not have multiple tape measures, draw chalk lines or cut some narrow fabric strips to create the outline. Although this might not be necessary for everyone, if I don't do this, the design drifts out of alignment, and I find myself constantly moving and shifting the folded filler fabrics.

Section off a design wall with tape measures.
Photo by author

I pinned Sketch #2 to the design wall and used it as my guide for block and filler fabric placement and size. I placed the sewn blocks on the design wall and started filling in the space around them by roughly folding uncut pieces of fabric to the approximate size according to my sketch. In this quilt, I folded all the fabrics to approximately 1½″ wide (grid value); their length was determined by the number of grids they occupied in the drawing (1 grid wide by 6 grids long is 1½″ × 9″).

> ◆◆◆◆◆◆ **Noteworthy** ◆◆◆◆◆◆
>
> Originally I had a different block design in the position where the Trip Around the World is now. The original block, once in place with the others, was too large, too light, and drew too much attention. I replaced it with the Trip Around the World block, using smaller pieces and lower contrast.

During this process, I made a couple more minor refinements and then drew a final Sketch #3, which reflects cutting numbers for each rectangle in the background. When this process was complete, I was thrilled with how my quilt looked (this takes considerable time for me, sometimes weeks). I carefully examined Sketch #3 to determine the sewing sequence. I looked for long seams and began making X's on sections that could be sewn independently. During this process, I sometimes add seamlines to simplify construction and then join the sections to complete the quilt top.

DRAFTING FOR THE CREATIVE QUILTER

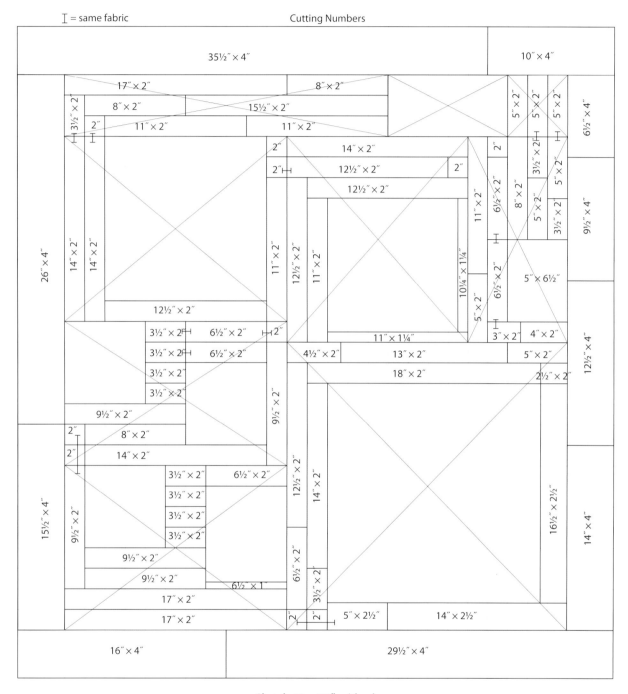

I = same fabric   Cutting Numbers

Sketch #3 – 1½″ grid value

Photo by author

Borders

Following the same process as the background, I folded and pinned fabric around the edge of the quilt, changing and refining until I was pleased. I wanted the borders to be dark and to blend with what they touched. I also pieced them in two or more fabrics and colors to quietly move color and help with the blending.

Progressive sequence working on design wall
Photo by author

Designing on an overall grid is a great way to begin designing your own quilts. It is logical, flexible, safe, and successful, whether you are an experienced quiltmaker or just beginning to create your own designs.

Photo by author

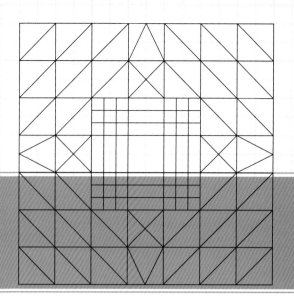

Designing within Traditional Blocks

For many years, I have used traditional patchwork blocks as a stepping stone to what some might describe as new or "original" block designs. Original design can be a slippery slope in traditional patchwork, because there are only so many ways to rearrange geometric shapes. I prefer to describe my work as "based on traditional patchwork," because as soon as I think I might have designed something new or original, it pops up in a magazine or book. Although I might not always be designing original work, fracturing the space of traditional blocks creates something unique and special to me.

Specifically, what I do is take a simple patchwork block I like, often stars, and fracture the shapes within that block into more shapes or replace shapes with different shapes. The more you break up or change space, the more design, color, fabric, and value opportunities are created. My experience has been to fracture the space of either grid-based blocks or 8-pointed star drafting category blocks, but you can use this design idea with any style of block you desire.

DESIGNING WITHIN GRID-BASED BLOCKS

Let's look at a simple Ohio Star block on a 3 × 3 grid. The four corner squares and the center square are empty; this is a great place to add shapes and create detail. The corner squares could be fractured into a square-in-a-square, points, half-square triangles, 9-patch units, and so on. The center could become another smaller Ohio Star block or any other block you'd like (because you now know how to divide any size square into any grid formation, pages 17–18).

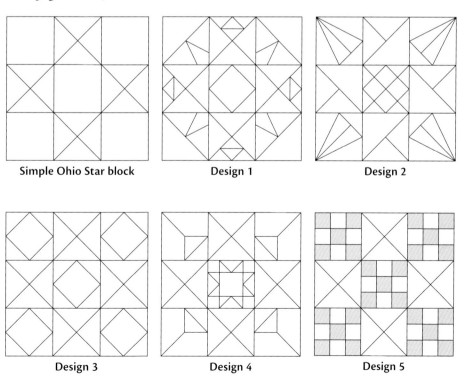

Simple Ohio Star block   Design 1   Design 2

Design 3   Design 4   Design 5

Any time you are working in traditional patchwork, see if you can fracture any of its existing space to create a unique design. It doesn't matter if the design already exists somewhere in the universe; it's new to you. However, if you plan on publishing it as "original," do some checking and adhere to all copyright rules and laws. You get the idea. Just one word of caution: Don't go overboard and create a chaotic design; do use good taste and good sense.

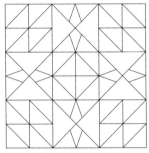

Chaotic design

When I do this process of fracturing, I first sketch or draw my block on graph paper. Then I begin my fracturing process, still somewhat roughly. I draw lines from corner to corner, midpoint to midpoint, intersection to intersection, or any combination of those. When I create these sketches, I can work on the whole block, or, if the block is symmetrical, I have the option of working with a part of it (½, ¼, ⅛) and then use mirrors to see the whole block design. Becoming familiar with what you're looking at when working with a partial design does take some getting used to. However, it saves time, gives you information, and allows you to see multiple design options on one line drawing or sketch.

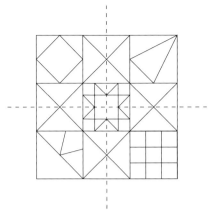

Four design options on one symmetrical block (Dashed lines indicate four mirror placements.)

Here are a couple grid-based traditional blocks you might be familiar with and some design ideas to fracture them. Sometimes I added lines or shapes, and other times I removed lines or shapes; sometimes I did both within the same design. Please feel free to use any of these blocks in your own work.

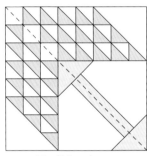
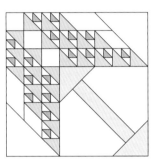

Traditional tree (Dashed line indicates mirror placement)   **Redesigned tree**

Detail

Autumn Window, 17" × 24", designed and pieced by the author.

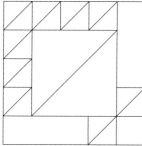
May basket

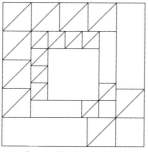
Draft smaller basket inside larger one

A second way you might redesign grid-based blocks is to add another row of grids. I used this idea when making the *Sampler Supreme* (page 99). I love the Goose in the Pond block, which is a 5 × 5 grid. I added another row of grids, which brings it to a 7 × 7 grid. I then made two minor changes to redesign the block. I ended up not using it in my quilt, but I will use the block some other time.

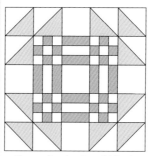
Goose in the Pond block

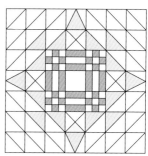
Redesigned Goose in the Pond block

DESIGNING WITHIN TRADITIONAL 8-POINTED STAR DRAFTING CATEGORY BLOCKS

◆◆◆ Noteworthy ◆◆◆

It is important that you have a clear understanding of the 8-pointed star drafting category in order to follow this process (page 44).

I enjoy the design process of fracturing existing shapes or removing shapes within designs in the 8-pointed star drafting category. This category is different from grid-based blocks, however, because the equality of 8-pointed star designs lies between the star points rather than in equal grids of squares across and down the block.

Shadow Baskets, 28" × 28", designed, pieced, and quilted by the author.

Detail

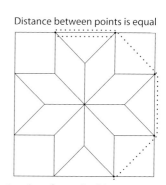

Grids are equal / Distance between points is equal

Grid-based drafting category / **8-pointed star drafting category**

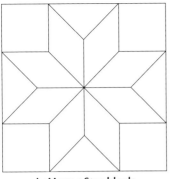

LeMoyne Star block

The LeMoyne Star block is the most basic of stars in this category, and it is versatile. If you take a simple LeMoyne Star and work with only one-eighth of the design and mirrors, you will be able to transform it from its humble beginnings to something spectacular. For example, if you fracture the eight diamonds of a LeMoyne Star, you can create a variety of blocks. They already exist in traditional patchwork, but that is how they were created.

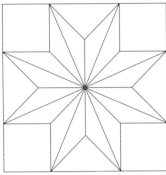

Silver and Gold block

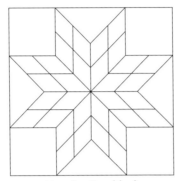

Morning Star block

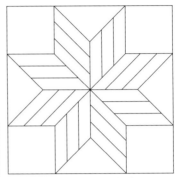

Liberty Star block

The following design transforms a LeMoyne Star into a Nosegay or Cornucopia block. To do this, I simply removed and added shapes.

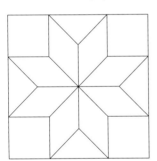

LeMoyne Star block

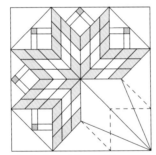

Redesigned into a Nosegay or Cornucopia block

Passion Flower, 22″ × 22″, designed, pieced, and quilted by the author.

Detail

DESIGNING THE 36″ SEDONA

The same three shapes—diamond, square, and triangle—that make up a LeMoyne Star make up a Carpenter's Wheel block. In fact, whatever size LeMoyne Star you make—let's say 6″—those three template shapes are the same size shapes you need for making a 12″ Carpenter's Wheel block. For the 36″ *Sedona* (page 116), I simply fractured the square, diamond, and triangle shapes of an 18″ LeMoyne Star. For the 18″ *Sedona*, I fractured the square, diamond, and triangle shapes of a 9″ LeMoyne Star.

To design *Sedona* (or you could redesign it), I began with a line drawing of a Carpenter's Wheel block that was about 6″ square. I knew I would make a 36″ design, but you do not have to know what size you're making to begin the designing process; you can choose or change size even after designing. You do not ever have to actually sew it; just begin to sketch and fracture the shapes with a small ruler or straight edge and a pencil. Your sketch does not need to be perfectly drawn. When I design, I'm only sketching and doodling and hopefully ending up with a new quilt design. I use the mirrors right on my paper to "see" the whole block.

♦♦♦♦ Noteworthy ♦♦♦♦

All templates are included for *Sedona* (page 116) for both the 36″ and the 18″ sizes.

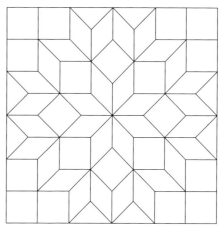

Drawing of a Carpenter's Wheel block

Drawings of a Carpenter's Wheel block with a variety of design possibilities. Mirrors can be placed on one-eighth of the design (the red lines) to show the entire block as it would appear if the design of this section were used for the whole block.

1. To create a smaller, third star in the center of a Carpenter's Wheel block, simply connect the corners of 4 squares across 2 diamonds (red lines), as well as the corners of the 4 squares on-point (blue lines). This creates 2 squares—one straight and one on-point—superimposed on top of each other.

Refer to the *Sedona* photo, page 116, as you follow the process.

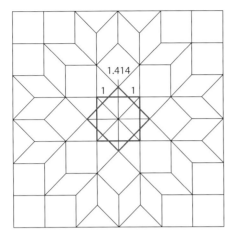

Create 2 squares—one straight and one on-point.

When you do this, the 1, 1.414, and 1 value divisions emerge, just like the top edge of a LeMoyne Star. This enables me to draft a new, smaller 8-pointed star (page 54).

2. Label the divisions A and B. Working clockwise from the top edge, connect each A to an opposite B and to a second B to create the small diamond and triangle, shaded in.

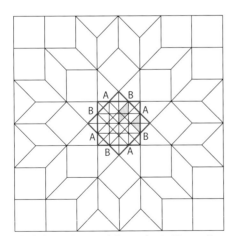

Label the points and draw the LeMoyne Star.

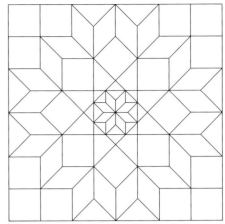

Erase all unnecessary lines, leaving only seamlines, to reveal a smaller 8-pointed star and 8 triangles

3. You can then fracture these new shapes. I fractured the large diamond into 4 smaller diamonds by finding the midpoint of all 4 sides and connecting them, sort of like a slanted 4-patch unit. Next, I fractured one of the inner diamonds again in the same way (green).

4. The triangles appear too large and out of proportion to the diamonds, so I fractured each triangle into 4 smaller triangles, giving additional color and fabric opportunities. Find the midpoint of each of the 3 sides of the triangle, connect those points to create a square, then divide the square in half diagonally. One triangle is now 4 (orange).

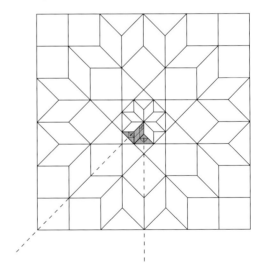

Redesigned diamond (green) and triangles (orange) fractured (The dashed line indicates mirror placement.)

5. Moving outward, split the kite shape vertically from point to point. In this example, I left the adjoining triangles plain (red). You do not have to fracture every shape.

6. To fracture the squares, go up equidistant from the corner points on both sides and connect those marks to the opposite corner, creating another long, slender point (blue). In my block, I just estimated this distance. To create continuity, I split the new point vertically, like the kite shape. This completes the center section. Be sure to keep placing the mirrors on your sketch to evaluate your design.

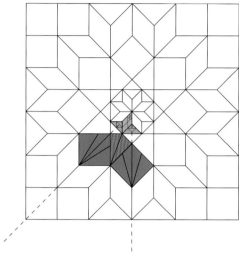

Fractured kite (red) and squares (blue)

7. Fracture the 24 outer diamonds that surround the center section in a similar way to create unity. Remember, unity is created through repetition.

8. Split one diamond in half horizontally. Then split the upper half of that diamond vertically. For the lower half, connect the midpoint of each side of the diamond's lower half to create another diamond and 2 triangles. Then fracture that diamond into 4 and fracture the inner diamond again into 4 smaller diamonds to echo the center. Repeat this fracturing process for a diamond on each side of this new diamond (3 total), so that when you place your mirrors on your drawing, you can see the whole *Sedona* developing.

9. Fracture the 16 outer triangles (aqua) by first creating 4 smaller triangles. The shapes will probably still seem too large, so fracture the inner triangle into 4 more smaller triangles; this also adds more detail.

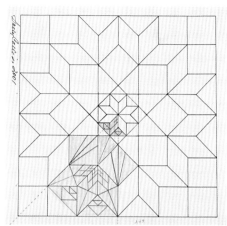

Redesigned outer diamonds (yellow) and outer triangles (aqua); *Sedona* complete

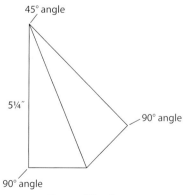

Mirrors on sketch

10. At this point, if you love your design, you would decide the size of block you wanted to make, if you do not already know. I wanted a 36″ block, so I needed to know the size of the diamond, square, and triangle for an 18″ LeMoyne Star block: 18″ ÷ 3.414 (sum of the parts) = 5.272″ = 5¼″. Referring to my sketch, I drafted each shape, using the 5¼″ size as my guide.

11. To draft the kite shape (red), draw 2 lines each 5¼″ long at a 45° angle from each other. Draw a line from each end at a 90° angle until they intersect.

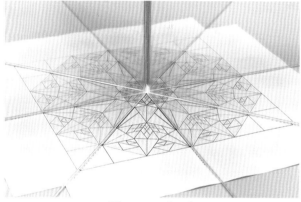

Draw a kite shape.

12. To draw the triangle (left unfractured) that joins to the kite, measure the short side of the kite shape and draw 2 lines of that measurement at a 90° angle to each other; connect their ends. This is the triangle shape.

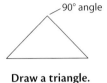

Draw a triangle.

13. To draw the square with the point (blue), draw a 5¼″ square and come up equidistant from the corner. Connect those points to the corner of the square.

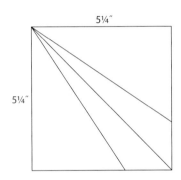

Draw a square.

14. All 4 small triangles together (orange) on each side of the center star diamonds make the same triangle shape that connects to the kite. To create the small triangles within that larger triangle, find and make a mark at the midpoint of each side of the triangle and connect them. This creates a square. Divide this small square diagonally. You now have the small triangles.

Create 4 small triangles.

♦♦♦♦ Noteworthy ♦♦♦♦

If you plan to make *Sedona* (see pages 116–126), refer to the process of how this small diamond unit (green) is created (see page 118). You will be pleasantly surprised at how easy it is to make; do not be deterred from making it.

15. All 4 sides of the center large diamond shape (green) are the same size as the short side of the triangle that connects to the kite. Find the midpoint of all 4 sides of the diamond and connect them. Now you have 4 smaller diamonds. Find the midpoint of each side of one of those diamonds and connect them to find the size of the very small diamond.

Create the center diamonds.

16. Each side of the outer diamonds (yellow) measures 5¼″. Draw a diamond with 4 sides all measuring 5¼″. Divide the diamond in half horizontally, then divide the upper half of the diamond vertically. Find and mark the midpoint of the 3 sides of the lower diamond and connect the marks. This creates a small diamond and 2 triangles. Find and mark the midpoint of the 4 sides of the diamond and connect them to create 4 small diamonds. Find and mark the midpoint of the inner small diamond and connect the marks to create 4 smaller diamonds.

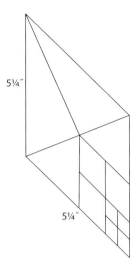

Outer diamonds

17. To fracture the outer triangles (aqua), find and mark the midpoint of all 3 sides, then connect them. This creates a square. Divide the square in half diagonally to create 4 triangles. Mark the midpoint of the 3 sides of the inner triangle. Connect those marks to create a square. Then divide the square in half diagonally to create 4 triangles. The large outer triangle is now fractured into 7 triangles.

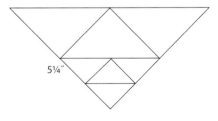

Triangles

Once you have drawn your shapes, make templates (page 90) and then create a color plan by making a rough-cut mock-up in actual size (page 91) using your templates.

MORE CARPENTER'S WHEEL DESIGNS

Following are four additional designs and a complete quilt (Tenacious), all created by fracturing the shapes of a Carpenter's Wheel structure in different ways.

Design #1; 18″ Carpenter's Wheel fractured

Tenacious, 23″ × 23″, designed, pieced, and quilted by the author; 9″ Carpenter's Wheel fractured.

Design #2

Design #3

Design #4

Redesigned Carpenter's Wheel Design #2 showing isolated shapes of square, triangle, and diamond

REDESIGNING A FEATHERED STAR BLOCK

The Feathered Star, a much loved and admired block for quiltmakers, is another block in the 8-pointed star drafting category, because the distance between its points are equal. I designed the center block of my quilt *Asian Influence* simply by fracturing some of the base shapes of a 15″ Radiant Feathered Star block (page 65), the simplest and most basic of the Feathered Stars.

Side-by-side: Radiant Feathered Star block and detail of *Asian Influence*

I began redesigning the Radiant Feathered Star on a 6″ line drawing of a Radiant Feathered Star block.

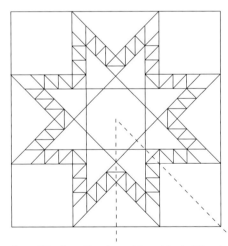

Line drawing of Radiant Feathered Star block (The dashed line indicates ⅛ of the design and mirror placement.)

1. I knew I would put something in the center octagon, but I was undecided at first, so I moved outward to the feathers. I decided to fracture one side of the half-square triangle feather unit. I simply broke the triangle into 4 triangles by connecting the midpoint of the 3 sides of the triangle. This created a small square, which I divided in half diagonally (shaded).

2. There are many ways to divide the kite shape. I decided to first create a diamond inside. To do that, I needed to find and mark the midpoint of the 2 long sides of the kite. I drew 2 lines at a 45° angle from the bottom point of the kite to the marks on the long sides of the kite. To fracture the new diamond into 4 smaller ones, I found the midpoint of each side of the diamond and connected those points to create 4 smaller ones (red). This process also created 2 triangles, one on each side of the diamond (blue).

3. Once I drew in ⅛ of the fractured feathers and the kite, I placed my mirrors so I could see the whole block. It became apparent that it would be easy to overdo this process and create chaos, because the fractured feathers create a lot of energy and demand a lot of attention. I tried fracturing the diamond at the tip of the kite shape but ended up leaving it as is. When I placed the mirrors around the design, I saw that it was getting a little busy and chaotic. You can fracture any and all shapes, but the idea is to create a beautiful design. The mirrors help me see the whole design and make informed decisions.

4. I then placed a point in the 4 triangles and divided the corner square in half diagonally to create 4 additional points. To create the point (green), I measured up 1″ from the 90° corner on both sides of the short sides of the triangles and connected them to the midpoint of the long side of the triangles to create another layer of star points.

5. Next was the center octagon. I first decided that I wanted my Feathered Star block to be 15″. I needed to figure out the size of the octagon. To do that, I used Feathered Star Drafting Method 2 (see page 67). The size of the center octagon for a 15″ Feathered Star is 4¼″. I decided to place a Wheel of Fortune block in the octagon with a LeMoyne Star in its center (page 64). I sketched the shapes I needed inside the octagon and used the mirrors to see the results.

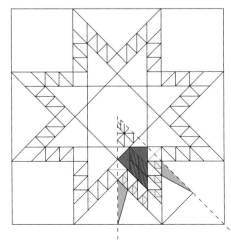

Steps 1–5: ⅛ of the redesigned Radiant Feathered Star block in *Asian Influence* (The dashed line indicates mirror placement for seeing the complete block.)

Line drawing of *Asian Influence*

Once you have a design you love, create your shapes, measure the new shapes, make templates, or, if they are ruler-friendly sizes, rotary-cut shapes (add ¼" seam allowance to all sides of each shape before cutting). Then create a color map using the rough-cut mock-up and mirror technique (page 91). Once you love the color and fabric placement, it's time to sew!

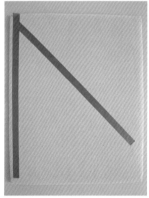

Use blue tape to create a 45° wedge.

Actual size fabric mock-up of ⅛ of design in place on wedge; place mirrors on edge of fabric to see whole block.

Mock-up with mirrors to see whole *Asian Influence* design

Asian Influence, 50″ × 50″, designed and pieced by the author; machine quilted by Lois Russell of San Diego, CA.

As you can see, 8-pointed stars are beautiful in and of themselves, but many are also suitable for redesigning. Designing on an overall grid or redesigning within traditional blocks are both simple and effective approaches. I encourage you to try for yourself. Even a small change in any block will nudge your creativity. The following are just some of the benefits of taking the time to design your own blocks:

- Create more of a challenge for yourself.
- Advance your creative skills and gain design experience.
- Learn new skills.
- Create more visual interest and detail in your work.
- Love your work when it's finished, with no guesswork!

There are many ways to change a design. You can add shapes, eliminate shapes, or change shapes. Don't forget to add appliqué if that's what you love. Appliqué would be perfect for the center octagon in the Feathered Star block. There is no risk—you have nothing to lose and everything to gain. Do not concern yourself with how you will sew, just design freely and enjoy the process.

Miscellaneous

TEMPLATES

Making Templates

Templates are wonderful, powerful tools that give high rewards and that improve our potential for both quality and custom work. Use templates if the shape you need is a size not easily cut with a rotary cutter and ruler or is oddly shaped or curved, if you want to custom cut a particular design area from a fabric, or if you want to custom cut from a strip unit. Accurate templates, which include ¼″ seam allowances, ensure accurate work. Templates support total freedom in design, they help align two pieces for sewing by pinning at reference dots marked on the fabric pieces, and they help monitor sewing accuracy because they reflect the sewing line. As you sew, place the template on the sewn units; the seamlines and the lines on the template should match. Also use templates to cut finished-size mock-up pieces when designing.

1. Place a manageable-size piece of ungridded, template plastic material over the shape needed. Be sure you have allowed adequate room to add a seam allowance. With a permanent black pen (do not use a Pigma Pen), mark a dot wherever a line changes direction; then, with a ruler edge, *almost* connect the dots, leaving them obvious and apparent for piercing or punching. This line between the dots is the sewing line you will use to place over your sewn work to monitor accuracy.

2. Write the identifying letter or number, block or design name, size, and grainline arrow on each template. These markings are very important, not only for the obvious informative reasons, but also because they identify the right side of the template.

3. To add ¼″ seam allowances on all sides of the shape and to cut it out of the plastic at the same time, remove the pattern from underneath the plastic and place the plastic on your cutting mat. Align the ¼″ line of the rotary cutting ruler so that it travels through the center of two dots along one edge of the shape. Position a small box cutter or X-acto knife next to the ruler's edge and score the plastic. Repeat for all lines and dots. Once the plastic is scored adequately, it will precisely crack off, resulting in an extremely accurate template that includes ¼″ seam allowances on all sides of the shape. If the shape has sharp or extended tips, trim them off.

4. Punch holes exactly over the dots, using a $1/16$″ hole punch, or place the template face down on a towel and carefully pierce the plastic at the dot with a stiletto or large needle by gently twisting, taking care not to crack the plastic. The hole should only be large enough to insert a pencil or marking tool so you can make a mark on the fabric.

5. Before using the templates to cut fabric, place the templates on the pattern and be sure the dots appear through your punched holes. Then, place appropriate template shapes onto one another, as if you were sewing, to make sure the edges and holes line up exactly. Do not cut fabric until your templates are accurate. If they do not line up in plastic, they will not line up as fabric.

Cutting Fabric with Templates

1. Place each template face down on the wrong side of the fabric; place reverse templates right side up. To prevent the templates from sliding and slipping on the fabric when cutting, roll small pieces of masking or painter's tape so it has double-stick capability and place it on the template.

2. With an appropriate fabric marker, mark dots through the punched holes onto the fabric.

3. Using an 18mm (small) rotary cutter and holding it like a pencil, carefully cut around the template, keeping the blade next to the edge of the plastic template. Use a small mat, so you can easily turn your work and cut comfortably. To prevent shaving your template edge, do not lift the cutter off the mat until you have completed cutting each edge. Even if you must stop to rearrange your hands on a long edge, leave the cutter blade in the mat. Lifting the cutter up and down is what results in shaving the template edge.

ROUGH-CUT MOCK-UP AND MIRRORS

I use mock-ups and mirrors as design tools to compose my work, piece by piece, and to interview color and placement in blocks or quilts before the actual cutting and sewing take place. Creating mock-ups is a creative, challenging, and exciting opportunity to explore ideas and compose your quilts without being encumbered by the sewing process. An important element of making mock-ups is recognizing that you do not have to be right the first time; just the last time. You must put something, anything, down first, and then begin to improve, compose, change, and follow your heart. It is an opportunity to explore the "what if" possibilities. What if I change red to blue, change the light to dark, change the floral fabric to a stripe?

Cut fabric for mock-ups the actual size without seam allowance, so you can more accurately evaluate how the colors and printed fabrics will look cut up and next to other colors and fabrics. A very small change can make a great difference.

If the block design is symmetrical, you only need to mock-up one-half, one-quarter, or one-eighth of the design and then use the mirrors to see the whole design.

If you're mocking up a rotary-cut design, determine the finished size of the shape (grid dimension tells you that, see pages 14–15) and then cut the shapes. For example, if the instructions say to cut 1½″ squares, you will cut 1″ squares for the mock-up. If you need half-square triangles, cut 1″ squares in half diagonally. Use a rotary cutter and ruler in these cases. If you're using templates, place the template on the fabric, mark dots through the punched holes, and then scissor cut or rotary cut from dot to dot. This does not need to be exact work, but it should be reasonably accurate or you will defeat the purpose.

Initially I work on a foamcore board covered with flannel (page 89). When working with larger designs, I transfer those pieces to the shiny side of freezer paper and press them into position with a piece of parchment paper or a pressing cloth. I then use that as my color map (not a construction map).

Pay attention to when your designs are symmetrical and take advantage of mock-up and mirrors in your design process. This is an exciting, challenging, useful, and creative technique. Explore. Have fun. It's not always where we are going or how fast we get there that matters as much as the road we take.

Pause, 16⅞" × 18", designed, pieced, and machine quilted by the author.

Pause

My goal was to create a simple, minimal, quiet design. I chose a favorite block, the Bear's Paw. But rather than arrange it in my usual traditional, predictable style (not that there's anything wrong with that!), I decided to step out of my box just a little and make some changes. First, I removed the bars that separate each paw in a traditional block, so I could use the paws individually. Then I added a smaller paw inside the larger one to add detail. Using a Sawtooth Star block as a structure, I placed individual paws in its corners and side triangles.

Then I created a center star design using the same half-square triangles and an on-point square. Once the block was sewn, I added plain fabric borders in different widths to create a more contemporary style, combined with 17 sawteeth and 3 small, individual paws for interest. I then strategically placed and appliquéd 15 squares on-point to add a little detail. My color and fabric choices reflected the quiet style I was after by keeping the value contrast lower than I usually use. I also chose fabric prints that were, for the most part, in character with my plan.

Vital Statistics

Block size: 2¼″ finished, 2¾″ unfinished (Double Paw)

Drafting category: 9-patch, 3 × 3 grid

Grid dimension: Small paw ½″, Large paw ¾″

Number of pieces: 19 (Double Paw)

⅛ of center block

Center block with mirrors

Fabric Requirements

The yardage is the total for each color family. An assortment of different values and visual textures for each color is the key to success.

- **Browns:** 1 yard total
- **Pinks/Burgundy:** ¾ yard total
- **Greens:** ⅓ yard total

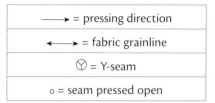

⟶	= pressing direction
⟵	= fabric grainline
⊘	= Y-seam
o	= seam pressed open

Cutting

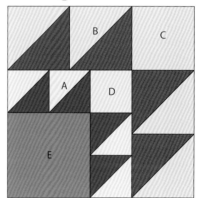

Double Paw block

For the 8 Double Paw blocks and the center star unit, you will need a total of 48 A's and 48 B's. They are created exactly the same, but then the A's are custom cut to 1″ and the B's are custom cut to 1¼″. To make the 8 Double Paws, arrange the appropriate A's and B's with the C-D-E squares and assemble as illustrated. You should have 16 A's and 16 B's left over for the center star unit. Cutting instructions for the A's and B's indicates the total amount; you must make individual quantity determinations based on your fabric and color choices.

Make templates (page 90) for H, I, J, K, and L (page 98). Turn over the I template for Ir (I reverse).

A: Cut 16 squares 2″ × 2″ from both background and paw fabrics for 32 total. Cut 8 squares 2″ × 2″ from both background and star point fabrics for 16 total.

B: Cut 16 squares 2″ × 2″ from both background and paw fabrics for 32 total. Cut 8 squares 2″ × 2″ from both background and star point fabrics for 16 total.

C: Cut 12 squares 1¼″ × 1¼″ from background fabric.

D: Cut 12 squares 1″ × 1″ from background fabric.

E: Cut 8 squares 1½″ × 1½″ from paw fabric.

F: Cut 1 square 2½″ × 2½″.

G: Cut 4 squares 1½″ × 1½″; then draw a line diagonally on the wrong side of each.

H: Cut 8.

I and Ir: Cut 4 of each.

J: Cut 4.

K: Cut 4.

Half-Square Triangles

1. Pair appropriate background and paw fabric A and B squares. Then draw a diagonal line on the lightest-color square of each pairing.

2. Sew ¼″ from the drawn line on both sides. Cut on the drawn line, press the seam open, and trim the seam allowance to a generous ⅛″. You should have 96 half-square triangle units.

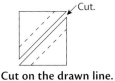

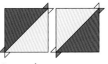

Draw a diagonal line and sew.   **Cut on the drawn line.**   **Press the seam open and trim.**

3. Based on your color fabric choices for A's and B's, custom cut a 1″ square from each A/A pairing and a 1¼″ square from each B/B pairing, to end up with 48 of each.

Custom cut 1″ A/A squares.   **Custom cut 1¼″ B/B squares.**

Double Bear's Paw Block
Arrange a complete block and assemble as shown. Make 8. Set aside.

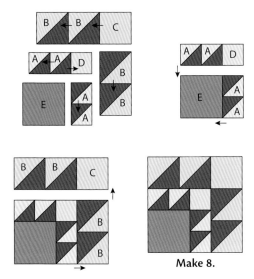

Make 8.

Center Star
1. Paying particular attention to the direction of the diagonal seams, make 8 pairs each of A's and B's.

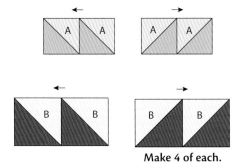

Make 4 of each.

2. Join 2 pairs of both A's and B's 4 times. Press the seams open.

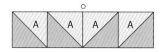

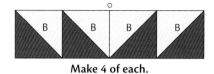

Make 4 of each.

3. Add a D to the ends of 2 A units.

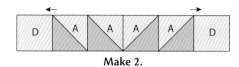

Make 2.

4. Add a C to the ends of 2 B units.

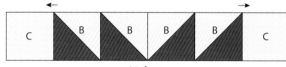

Make 2.

On-Point Square Unit

1. Place a G square over 1 corner of the F square. Sew right next to the line on the side that will be trimmed off.

2. Trim the excess.

3. Press toward G. Repeat for the 3 remaining corners. This center FG unit must measure 2½″ × 2½″ when complete.

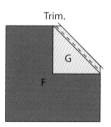

Sew on the scrap side of the line.   **Trim.**

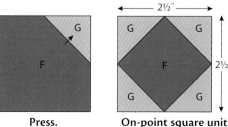

Press.   **On-point square unit**

Sawtooth Star

1. Arrange and assemble the FG unit, A units, and AD units.

2. Arrange the B units and BC units around the ADFG star and assemble. The block should measure 5″ × 5″ unfinished.

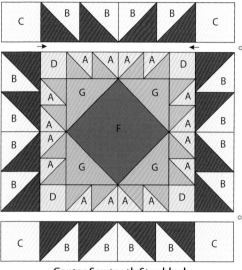

Center Sawtooth Star block

SIDE UNITS

1. Sew an I and an Ir to the 2 top edges of a Double Bear's Paw block; make 4.

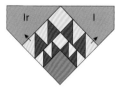

Partial side unit; make 4.

2. Add an H triangle to each of the 2 remaining edges of the Double Bear's Paw block; make 4.

Complete side unit; make 4.

CORNER UNITS

Add a J and a K to 4 Double Bear's Paw blocks.

Complete corner unit; make 4.

ASSEMBLY

1. Arrange 4 side units, 4 corner units, and a center star unit into 3 rows. Join units into Row 1, Row 2, and Row 3.

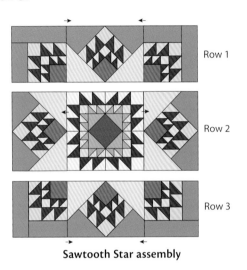

Sawtooth Star assembly

2. Join rows into the completed star. The block should measure 10⅞″ finished and 11⅜″ unfinished.

Complete star

Borders

1. Do not precut the border strips. Measure your quilt, one border at a time. The numbers are based on having sewn the block exactly. If your block measurements are different from mine, measure and use your own numbers from this point forward.

  DRAFTING FOR THE CREATIVE QUILTER

2. Nine separate borders will be added to the center star design. Some borders consist of only 1 fabric, while others add more fabrics and/or piecing. The piecing consists of 3 small Paw blocks and 17 sawteeth. Borders will be created and applied in numerical order.

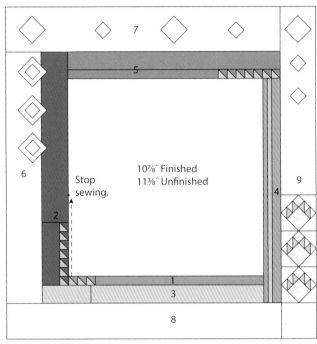

Quilt Border Assembly

SAWTEETH

You will need 17 sawteeth for 3 partially pieced borders and 12 additional sawteeth for the 3 small Bear's Paw blocks.

1. Cut 9 squares 2″ × 2″ from each of 2 fabrics for the sawteeth borders. This will yield 18 sawteeth; you only need 17. Pair one square from each fabric and draw a diagonal line on the wrong side of the lightest square of each pairing.

2. Cut 12 squares 2″ × 2″ for the small Bear's Paw blocks—6 from the background fabric and 6 from the paw fabric. Pair one square from each fabric and draw a diagonal line on the wrong side of the lightest square of each pairing.

3. Refer to page 94 to create the A size (1″) sawteeth.

BORDER 1

Shown as pink in the Quilt Border Assembly (above).

1. Join 3 sawtooth units together and press the seams open.

2. Cut a 1″ × 9⅞″ strip and join it to the 3 sawtooth units; press toward the strip.

3. Add Border 1 to the bottom edge of the block and press toward the border.

BORDER 2

Shown as blue in the Quilt Border Assembly (page 96).

1. Join 7 sawtooth units together and press the seams open.

2. Cut a 1¼″ × 4″ strip of fabric and join it to the 7 sawtooth units; press toward the fabric strip.

3. Cut a 1¾″ × 9⅝″ strip of fabric. Add it to the sawtooth unit and press toward the fabric strip.

4. Add Border 2 to the left side of the quilt. Start sewing at the sawtooth end and stop sewing an inch or so past the sawteeth. This partial seam will be completed after you add Border 5.

BORDER 3

Shown as yellow in the Quilt Border Assembly (page 96).

1. Cut a 1½″ × 2¾″ strip of fabric.

2. Cut a 1½″ × 10⅜″ strip of fabric.

3. Sew the 2 strips together, end to end, and press the seam open.

4. Add Border 3 to the bottom of the quilt.

BORDER 4

Shown as green in the Quilt Border Assembly (page 96).

This border consists of three strips sewn together and then added to the quilt as one. Cut and sew them together exactly as explained to reveal the ⅛″ strip. Do not mix up the strip number or their order of sewing once you have cut them. You cannot move them around.

1. Cut Strip 1 to ¾″ × 13½″.

2. Cut Strip 2 to 1″ × 13½″.

3. Cut Strip 3 to 1⅜″ × 13½″.

4. Sew Strip 1 to Strip 2 and press the stitches. Trim the ¼″ seam allowance to an exact ⅛″ by placing the ⅛″ line of the ruler over the thread line and trimming away the excess seam allowance. Press toward Strip 2.

5. Pair Strip 1–2 with Strip 3, with Strip 3 on the bottom. Align the edges of Strips 2 and 3, but sew next to the just-trimmed seam allowance. Sew straight and slowly. How well you cut and sew is how straight and even the ⅛″ strip will be.

6. Press the stitches, trim the excess seam allowance to within ⅛″ of the last line of stitches, and press toward Strip 3.

7. Cut this strip unit to 12⅞″ and add it to the right side of the quilt.

BORDER 5

Shown as orange in the Quilt Border Assembly (page 96).

1. Sew 7 sawtooth units together and press the seams open.

2. Cut 1 strip of fabric 1″ × 8¾″, join it to the sawtooth, and press toward the strip.

3. Cut 1 strip 1¼″ × 12¼″, add it to the sawtooth strip, and press toward the plain strip. Add this to the top of the quilt.

Noteworthy: Now align the free edge of Border 2 to the quilt edge and complete the partial seam.

BORDER 6

Cut 1 strip of fabric 2¼″ × 14⅛″ and add it to the left side of the quilt.

BORDER 7

Cut 1 strip of fabric 3⅛″ × 15¼″ and add it to the top of the quilt.

BORDER 8

Cut 1 strip of fabric 2¼″ × 15¼″ and add it to the bottom of the quilt.

BORDER 9

This border is created in three sections: a bottom rectangle, a top rectangle, and three small Bear's Paw blocks.

1. Make a template for L (page 98).

2. Cut 1 top rectangle 2⅝″ × 10⅜″.

3. Cut 1 bottom rectangle 2⅝″ × 2¼″.

4. A: Use the 12 sawtooth units, 4 for each paw, created in Steps 2 and 3 of Sawteeth, page 96.

5. E: Cut 3 squares 1½″ × 1½″ from the paw fabric for bear paws.

6. D: Cut 3 squares 1″ × 1″ from the background for bear paws.

7. L: Cut 12 L triangles, from the background, 4 for each bear paw.

8. Lay out 1 paw and assemble as shown.

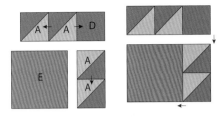

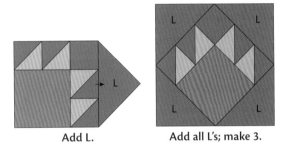

Make 3.

9. Add an L to each side of the 3 paws.

Add L.   Add all L's; make 3.

10. Join the 3 paws together and press the seams open. Add the paws to the top and bottom rectangles.

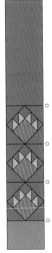

Join the paws and add to the rectangles.

11. Add Border 9 to the right side of the quilt.

Appliquéd On-Point Squares

You will need 6 squares 1″ × 1″ for the borders, 11 squares ½″ × ½″ for the borders, and Double Bear's Paws in the star, and 1 square ¾″ × ¾″ for the center.

1. See pages 112–113 for complete appliqué preparation and process instructions. See the quilt photo (page 92) for placement.

2. Appliqué the squares to the quilt surface.

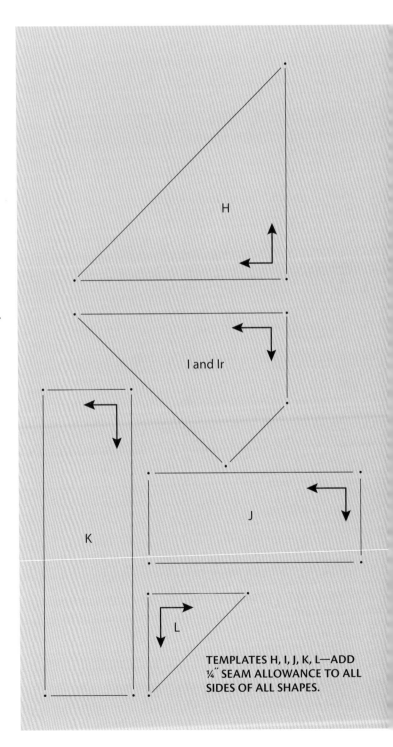

TEMPLATES H, I, J, K, L—ADD ¼″ SEAM ALLOWANCE TO ALL SIDES OF ALL SHAPES.

DRAFTING FOR THE CREATIVE QUILTER

Sampler Supreme, 44½" × 47½", designed, appliquéd, and pieced by the author; machine quilted by Lois Russell of San Diego, CA.

Sampler Supreme

It seemed obvious to choose a sampler quilt as one of the projects for this drafting book. I wanted to offer a project that incorporated a variety of block designs and opportunities for you to create a unique, individual quilt. I chose eight different block designs, a variety of drafting categories, and, in the end, six different block sizes. Instead of choosing my predictable (and much loved) traditional setting, I arranged the blocks within a grid format (refer to the Design Chapter on page 69) to give the quilt a more contemporary feel.

The primary focus for sampler quilts is the blocks. The background or setting should quietly enhance the blocks without overpowering them. I used a mixture of blues, teals, magentas, and golds in many different values and visual textures. I made the blocks first and then placed them on the design wall. I filled in the area around the blocks with colors and values of fabrics that complemented the blocks. I wanted the color to move over the quilt in waves of color, blending smoothly from one color to another. I created a smooth transition between fabric and color changes through sameness of value, which also helps camouflage seams. I placed the largest block and the darkest values (weight) at the bottom to create visual balance.

Although the complete pattern for *Sampler Supreme* is included, I encourage you to change anything you like to make it uniquely yours. For each block, I've given you the drafting category so you can refer back to the drafting instructions and make size changes. Here are some ideas to make simple changes:

- Change any or all block designs.

- Change the size of any or all block designs.

- Change the placement of the blocks within the grid space.

- Change the grid composition from rectangles to all squares or all triangles or a combination of shapes.

- Change the grid size.

- Change the number of blocks.

- Change the borders.

As each block is introduced, I have included a dashed line on the block diagram, where relevant, to indicate mirror placement as well as to isolate the area (½, ¼, or ⅛ of the design) to create a rough-cut mock-up in actual size (page 91). The 3-Dimensional Cube, 10-Pointed Star, and Chrysanthemum blocks were mocked up in their entirety (not shown).

Whether you make *Sampler Supreme* exactly as presented or change it up a bit, have fun!

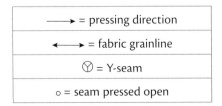

⟶ = pressing direction
⟷ = fabric grainline
⦵ = Y-seam
o = seam pressed open

Fabric Requirements

I used four color families and 50 to 60 different fabrics. A variety of values and visual textures for each color is the key to smoothly changing from one color to another. Fabric yardage listed is the total for each color.

- **Purples/Magentas:** 2½ yards total

- **Blues:** ¾ yard total

- **Golds/Yellows:** 1½ yard total

- **Teals:** 1 yard total

Corn and Beans Block

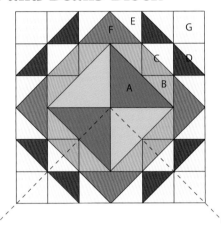

Corn and Beans block (Dashed line indicates mirror placement.)

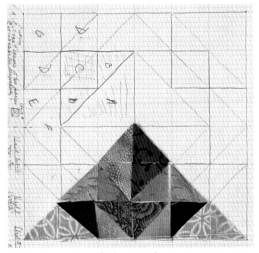

¼ design mock-up

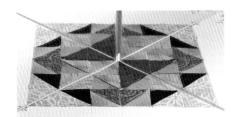

Mock-up with mirrors

Vital Statistics

Block size: 6″ finished,
6½″ unfinished

Drafting category: 9-patch,
6 × 6 grid

Grid dimension: 1″

Number of pieces: 52

CUTTING

A: Cut 1 square 4″ × 4″ from each of blue and light teal; cut into quarters diagonally.

B: Cut 8 squares 1½″ × 1½″ from light pink.

C: Cut 2 squares 2″ × 2″ from each of light blue and yellow; cut in half diagonally.

D: Cut 4 squares 2″ × 2″ from each of magenta and yellow; cut in half diagonally.

E: Cut 8 squares 1½″ × 1½″ of yellow; draw a diagonal line on the wrong side of each.

F: Cut 4 rectangles 1½″ × 2½″ from medium pink.

G: Cut 4 squares 1½″ × 1½″ from yellow.

PIECING

A Units

1. Pair 2 A triangles, 1 from each fabric. Make 2.

2. Join the 2 pairs.

Unit A; make 1.

BB/C Units

1. Trim the B squares ¼″ from 2 diagonal corners. Make 8.

B triangles; make 8.

2. Sew 2 C triangles, 1 from each fabric. Make 4. Custom cut 1 square 1½″ × 1½″ from each.

Custom cut; make 4.

3. Add a B triangle to 2 sides of each C half-square triangle. Make 4.

Add B's to C's; make 4.

D/D Units

Pair 2 D triangles, 1 from each fabric. Make 8. Custom cut 1 square 1½″ × 1½″ from each.

Custom cut; make 8.

EE/F Units

1. Sew an E square to an F rectangle diagonally. Sew, as shown, right next to the drawn line on the side that will be trimmed off. Trim out the E square's triangle only, leaving the rectangle in place.

2. Add a second E square as in Step 1; make 4.

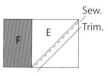

Sew.

Trim.

Press.

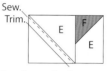

Sew from the bottom edge to the corner.

Trim.

Press; make 4.

ASSEMBLY

1. Add 4 BBC units to the A unit.

2. Join 2 DD units to 1 EEF unit; make 4.

3. Add 2 G's to 2 DDEEFDD units; make 2.

4. Assemble as shown.

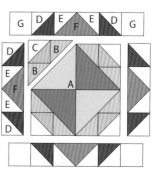

Corn and Beans assembly

Sawtooth Star Variation Block

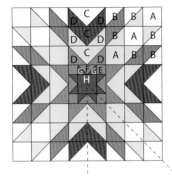

Sawtooth Star Variation block (Dashed line indicates mirror placement.)

⅛ design mock-up

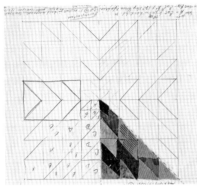

Mock-up with mirrors

Vital Statistics

Block size: 6″ finished, 6½″ unfinished

Drafting category: 4-patch, 8 × 8 grid

Grid dimension: ¾″

Number of pieces: 113

CUTTING

A: Cut 8 squares 1¼″ × 1¼″ from yellow and 4 squares 1¼″ × 1¼″ from light teal.

B: You need 24 (total) pairings of B's—8 blue/yellow, 8 dark teal/yellow, and 8 light teal/dark teal. For each color pairing, cut 1 strip 2″ × 10″ of each fabric, place right sides together, and press. (Do not sew the strip pairings together.) From each strip pairing, cut 4 squares 2″ × 2″, and then cut in half diagonally.

C: Cut 4 rectangles 1¼″ × 2″ from each of yellow, dark pink, and light teal.

D: Cut 8 squares 1¼″ × 1¼″ from dark pink, 8 squares 1¼″ × 1¼″ from light teal, and 8 squares 1¼″ × 1¼″ from light pink; draw a diagonal line on the wrong side of each.

E: Cut 4 squares ⅞″ × ⅞″ from light pink.

F: Cut 4 rectangles ⅞″ × 1¼″ from light pink.

G: Cut 8 squares ⅞″ × ⅞″ from dark blue.

H: Cut 1 square 1¼″ × 1¼″ from dark blue.

PIECING

B/B Unit

Sew together 24 pairs of triangles. Custom cut 1 square 1¼″ × 1¼″ from each for a total of 24 BB units, with 8 of each color pairing.

BB unit; make 24.

C/DD Unit

1. Sew a D square to a C rectangle diagonally. Sew, as shown, right next to the drawn line on the side that will be trimmed off. Trim away only the D square's triangle, leaving the rectangle in place. Add a second D square similarly; make 12.

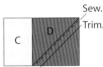

Sew.

Trim D only.

Press.

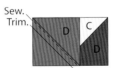

Sew from the bottom edge to the corner.

Trim D only.

Press. Make 12 CDD and 4 FGG.

F/GG Unit

Sew 2 G squares to 1 F rectangle; make 4, following the same process as for the CDD unit.

Corner Units

Join 6 BB units to 3 A squares; make 4.

Corner unit; make 4.

Side Units

Join 3 CDD units; make 4.

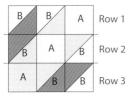

Side unit; make 4.

Center Star Unit

Arrange 4 E squares, 4 FGG units, and a center H square. Join units into 3 rows, and then join rows into a center star.

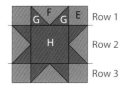

Center star unit; make 1.

ASSEMBLY

1. Arrange all the units. Join 2 AB corner units to a CDD side unit; make 2 (Rows 1 and 3).

2. Join 2 CDD side units to the center star (Row 2).

3. Join the 3 rows into the completed block.

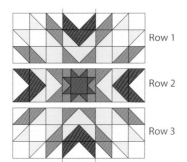

Sawtooth Star Variation assembly

3-D Cube Block

This block was inspired by a piece of fabric that had what looked like a six-sided cube printed all over its surface. I first created this block in one color, but then decided to use three colors—purple, teal, and pink. The degree of light, medium, and dark value must be the same for each color to really make this block appear as if you can see through it.

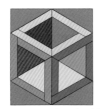

3-Dimensional Cube block

Design mock-up

Vital Statistics

Block size: 6″ × 7″ finished, 6½″ × 7½″ unfinished

Drafting category: Hexagon

Grid dimension: N/A

Number of pieces: 22

CUTTING

Make a template (page 90) for shapes A, B, C, and D (Dr is the reverse of D).

A: Cut 1 from each of dark purple, medium purple, medium teal, light teal, dark pink, and light pink.

B: Cut 2 from each of light purple, dark teal, and medium pink.

C: Cut 2 from each of light purple, dark teal, and medium pink.

D: Cut 2 from gold.

Dr: Cut 2 from gold.

PIECING

Make 6 ABC units: 2 purple, 2 teal, and 2 pink. Match dots and sew from edge to edge. Press away from A.

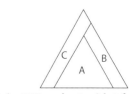

Join ABC; make 6, with 2 from each color.

Purple

1. Join a medium A to a light B and a light C.

2. Join a dark A to a light B and a light C.

Teal

1. Join a medium A to a dark B and a dark C.

2. Join a light A to a dark B and a dark C.

Pink

1. Join a dark A to a medium B and a medium C.

2. Join a light A to a medium B and a medium C.

ASSEMBLY

1. Join the purple medium/light ABC unit to the teal medium/dark ABC unit. Add the teal light/dark ABC unit. Press the seams open.

2. Join the purple dark/light ABC unit to the pink dark/medium ABC unit. Add the pink light/medium ABC unit. Press the seams open.

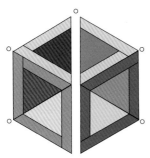

Join 3 ABC units; make 2.

3. Join the 2 units and press the seams open.

4. Add a D to 2 opposite corners of the unit from Step 3. Add a Dr to the remaining 2 corners.

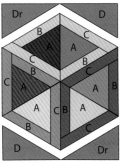

Add D and Dr.

3-DIMENSIONAL CUBE TEMPLATE PATTERNS; ADD ¼" SEAM ALLOWANCE TO ALL SIDES OF ALL SHAPES.

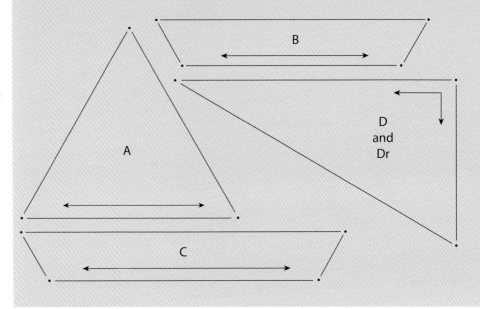

Setting Sun

This block comprises two Liberty Fan blocks.

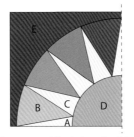

Liberty Fan block (Dashed line indicates mirror placement.)

½ design mock-up

Mock-up with mirrors

CUTTING

Make templates (page 90) for A, B, C, D, E, F, and G (page 105). Turn template over for Ar (reverse).

A and Ar: Cut 1 of each from yellows.

B: Cut 8 from pinks.

C: Cut 7 from yellows.

D: Cut 1 from yellow.

E: Cut 1 from dark pink.

F: Cut 4 from blue.

G: Cut 4 from blue.

PIECING

1. Sew a B to a C; make 7.

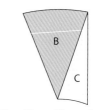

Sew B's to C's; make 7.

DRAFTING FOR THE CREATIVE QUILTER

2. Join the BC units. Add the remaining B to the right end of the point unit.

Add last B.

3. Add an A and Ar to each end of the point unit.

Add A and Ar.

4. Add D to the inside edge of the point unit.

5. Add E to the outside edge of the point unit.

6. To add bias detail, cut a teal piece of bias 1″ × 10″; then press it in half lengthwise, wrong sides together. With a small stitch length, sew ⅛″ from the fold.

7. Insert the ⅛″ bias bar, trim the seam allowance, and then move the seam allowance to a flat side of the bar. Dampen, press dry, and let cool. Remove the bar.

8. Leaving short tails at both ends, lightly glue baste the bias in place; then hand appliqué both edges. Trim the tails even with the block edge.

9. Appliqué 4 F and 4 G circles to the B pieces following the appliqué directions on pages 112–113. Refer to the photo on page 99 for placement.

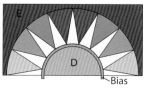

Add D, E, and bias detail.

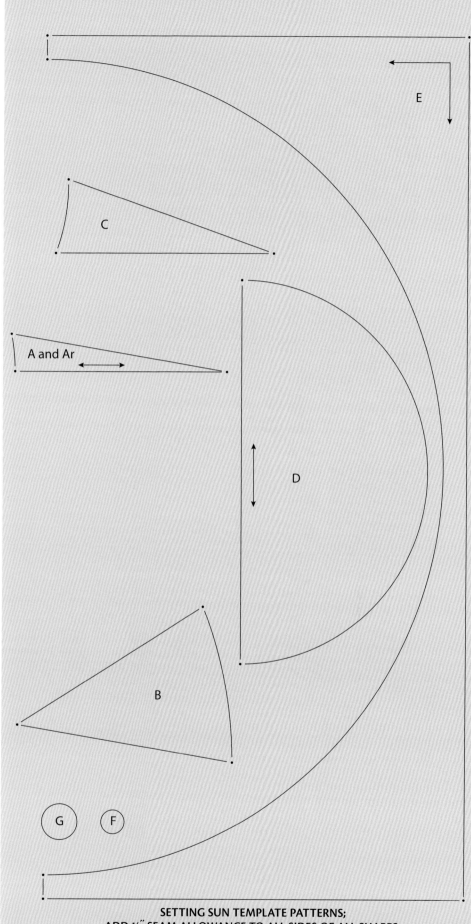

**SETTING SUN TEMPLATE PATTERNS;
ADD ¼″ SEAM ALLOWANCE TO ALL SIDES OF ALL SHAPES.**

Trip Around the World

Row 1

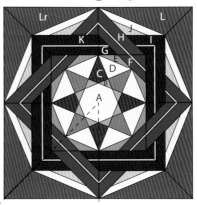

Trip Around the World block (Dashed lines indicate mirror placement.)

¼ design mock-up

Mock-up with mirrors

Vital Statistics

Block size: 9¾″ finished, 10¼″ unfinished

Drafting category: 13 × 13 grid

Grid dimension: ¾″

Number of pieces: 181

◆◆◆ Noteworthy ◆◆◆

For the mock-up, cut ¾″ squares into quarters diagonally for the center star points and cut ¾″ squares for the remaining squares.

CUTTING

A: Cut 1¼″ × 1¼″ squares: 1 dark teal, 32 yellow, 12 light blue, 16 dark blue, 20 purple, 24 red-violet, 20 light teal, 16 magenta, 12 dark pink, 8 light pink, and 4 medium pink.

B: Cut 2½″ × 2½″ squares: 2 dark pink, 1 light teal, and 1 yellow; then cut each into quarters diagonally.

PIECING

Star Point Unit

1. Arrange 1 star point unit.

2. Sew together a light teal and a dark pink triangle; press. Make 4. Sew together a yellow and a dark pink triangle; press. Make 4.

3. Join pairs of triangles to complete the unit; press open. Make 4.

Sew 2 triangles together; make 8. Join pairs.   **Star point unit; make 4.**

4. Custom cut 1 square 1¼″ × 1¼″ from each star point unit.

Custom cut squares.

5. Arrange all A squares and star point units.

---

6. Join squares and star point units into rows. Press the seams of Row 1. Press the seams of Row 2 opposite Row 1. Press the seams of all odd-numbered rows the same as Row 1 and all even-numbered rows the same as Row 2. Join the rows.

Interlocking Squares

Interlocking Squares block (Dashed lines indicate mirror placement.)

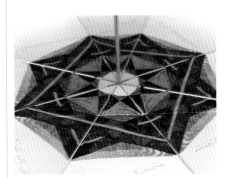

⅛ design mock-up

Mock-up with mirrors

Vital Statistics

Block size: 12″ finished, 12½″ unfinished

Drafting category: 8-pointed star

Grid dimension: N/A

Number of pieces: 73

COLOR AND DESIGN

It is important that you create high contrast between the two colors that create the interlocking squares to enhance the interlocking pattern. I have included an additional template (A1) in case you want to replace the A octagon shape with eight A1 wedge shapes. These wedges could be cut from a border print to create an interesting design or from a stripe fabric or from a strip unit.

CUTTING

Make templates (page 90) for shapes A, B, C, D, E, F, G, H, I, J, K, L (pages 108–109). Turn template over for Lr (reverse).

A: Cut 1 from yellow *or* A1: Cut 8 from selected fabric.

B: Cut 8 from light teal.

C: Cut 4 from magenta and 4 from purple.

D: Cut 8 from yellow.

E: Cut 8 from blue.

F: Cut 4 from a teal/yellow/teal strip unit.

G: Cut 4 from a magenta/yellow/magenta strip unit.

H: Cut 4 from a teal/yellow/teal strip unit.

I: Cut 4 from a magenta/yellow/magenta strip unit. Cut 4 from a teal/yellow/teal strip unit.

J: Cut 8 from a pink/yellow strip. Cut 2 strips 1¼″ × 1¼″ from each of pink and yellow.

K: Cut 4 from a magenta/yellow/magenta strip unit.

L and Lr: Cut 4 of each from purples.

The following explains exactly how to include the ⅛″ accent detail in shapes F, G, H, I, and K. These shapes are created in exactly the same way; follow the directions carefully. Make four strip units: two in magenta/yellow/magenta and two in teal/yellow/teal. Once these are made, place the appropriate template shape on the appropriate strip unit and cut.

Strip 1: Cut 2 strips 1¾″ × 40″ from each of magenta and teal.

Strip 2: Cut 4 strips 1″ × 40″ from accent yellow.

Strip 3: Cut 2 strips 1¾″ × 40″ from each of magenta and teal.

Strip unit: magenta

PIECING THE STRIP UNITS

1. Sew a magenta to an accent strip, right sides together.

2. Trim the seam allowance to an exact ⅛″ by placing the ⅛″ line of a ruler over the thread line and trimming away the excess ⅛″. It is much easier to do this with a short ruler or a 4″ square ruler. When you need to advance the short ruler, leave the cutter blade in the mat to ensure a smooth cut edge over the entire length.

3. Press the seam allowance toward Strip 2 in accent yellow.

4. Place Strip 3 right side up. Place Strip 1–2 on top of Strip 3, right sides together. Align their edges as usual, but sew next to the previously trimmed seam allowance edge.

5. Press toward Strip 3. After evaluating, trim the seam allowance to ¼″ from the last line of stitching.

6. Repeat Steps 1–5 for a second magenta/yellow/magenta strip unit and then for 2 teal/yellow/teal strip units.

7. Place templates F, G, H, I, and K on the appropriate strip unit, aligning lines on the template with the seams of the strip unit; cut out.

8. Sew a pink to a yellow strip, right sides together. Trim seam allowance to ⅛″, and press seam open. Repeat for a second pink/yellow strip unit. Align line on template J with the seam on the strip unit, and cut out.

PIECING THE BLOCK UNITS

Make 5 units: 1 ABBBB (Unit 1), 4 BCCDE (Unit 2), 2 BCCDDDEEE (Unit 3), 4 GHIJL (Unit 4), and 4 KJILr (Unit 5). Pin at the dots to align the shapes; then sew edge to edge.

Unit 1

Join 4 B's to the A octagon.

Unit 1; make 1.

Unit 2

1. Join C to B and then another C to D. Join CB to CD; add E. Make 4.

Unit 2; make 4.

2. To Unit 1, add 2 Unit 2's to create Row 2 of the center star.

Unit 3

To Unit 2, add 2 D's and 2 E's. Make 2. (These are Rows 1 and 3 of the center star.)

Unit 3; make 2.

♦♦♦ Noteworthy ♦♦♦

I did not add the L and Lr shapes when making Units 4 and 5 until I was working on the design wall and could decide which fabric and color to use at each corner of the block to blend into the background.

Unit 4

Join G to H and I to J. Join GH to IJ. Add L. Make 4.

Unit 4; make 4.

Unit 5

Join I to J; add K. Add Lr. Make 4.

Unit 5; make 4.

ASSEMBLY

1. Join the 3 rows to create an octagon.

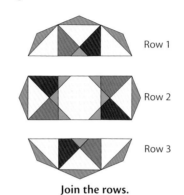

Join the rows.

2. Add 4 F triangles to square the octagon.

Center star

3. Join Unit 4 to Unit 5; make 4.

Join Unit 4 to Unit 5; make 4.

4. Add a Unit 4–5 to each side of the center star. Pin at the dots. Stop and start stitching at the dots, backstitching at both ends.

5. Sew the 4 corner seams, pinning at the dots. Sew from the outside corner's edge to the dot; then backstitch.

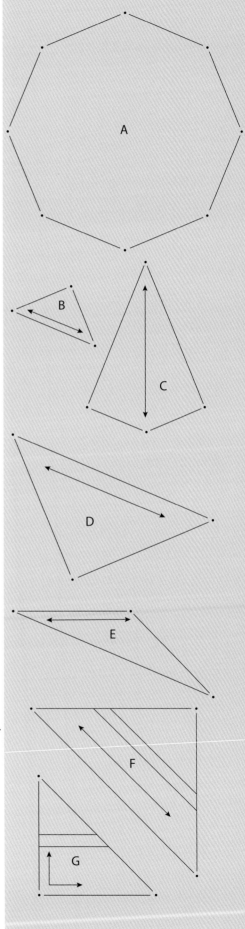

A1

K

L and Lr

I

J

H

INTERLOCKING SQUARE TEMPLATE PATTERNS; ADD ¼" SEAM ALLOWANCE TO ALL SIDES OF ALL SHAPES.

10-Pointed Star Block

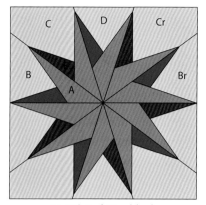

10-Pointed Star block

Vital Statistics

Block size: 6″ finished, 6½″ unfinished

Drafting category: 10-pointed star

Grid dimension: N/A

Number of pieces: 30

CUTTING

Make templates (page 90) for A, B, C, D, and E (patterns on page 110). Turn templates B and C over for Br and Cr (reverse).

A: Cut 5 from pink and 5 from teal.

B and Br: Cut 2 of each from background.

C and Cr: Cut 2 of each from background.

D: Cut 2 from background.

E: Cut 5 from magenta and 5 from dark teal.

PIECING

1. Arrange the block and assemble half of the block in 5 sections. Repeat for the second half.

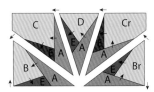 

Make 2 halves.

2. Join the 2 halves. Press this long seam open in the middle area. Clip and press in the direction of the arrows at the 2 ends of the seam.

Join the halves, clip, and press.

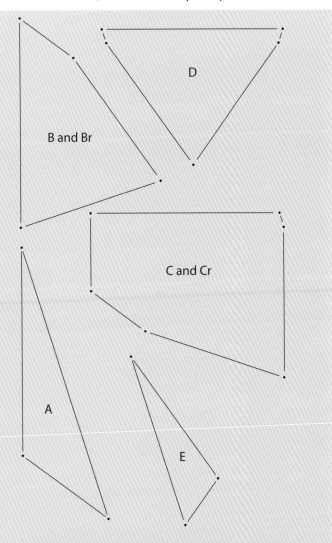

10-POINTED STAR TEMPLATE PATTERNS; ADD ¼˝ SEAM ALLOWANCE TO ALL SIDES OF ALL SHAPES.

Chrysanthemum

This block, inspired by a quilt by Kitty Pippin, is based on a mathematical formula of 12 divisions of a circle and spiraling squares (see Bibliography, page 127). The size of each square is the diagonal measurement of the square that precedes it. How you position your color can create either a concentric effect, as I did, or a spiraling effect.

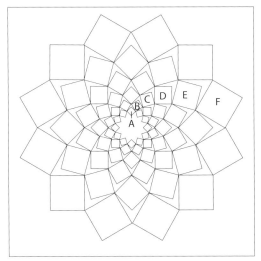

Chrysanthemum block

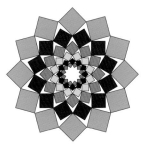 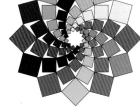

Color placed concentrically   **Color placed in a spiraling effect**

Vital Statistics

Block size: 16˝ finished, 16½˝ unfinished

Drafting category: N/A

Grid dimension: N/A

Number of pieces: 114

✦✦✦ Noteworthy ✦✦✦

Every step must be done exactly and accurately.

Do not press the block after marking.

DRAFTING FOR THE CREATIVE QUILTER

BACKGROUND PREPARATION

1. Trace the sectioned circle pattern (below) onto a plain piece of paper and cut out.

2. Cut a square of background fabric exactly 18″ square. This is larger than what you need; you will trim it later.

3. Find the midpoint of each side (9″) and draw a vertical and horizontal line to connect those midpoints. This identifies the center and divides the square into quarters.

4. Place the sectioned circle pattern on the fabric square by pinning through the paper center and into the center of the fabric. Do this on a rotary mat or a piece of cardboard. Keeping the centers matched with the pin, swivel the paper circle so the horizontal and vertical lines of the paper match the 4 lines marked on the fabric. Use removable tape to attach the paper circle to the fabric.

••• Noteworthy •••

I used a white Clover pen, which can be removed later with the heat of an iron but which will remain clear as you work. You must be able to see all the marked lines on the fabric for accurate placement of all the squares. If you are working on a white fabric, mark with a product you can see but can be removed later. Do not use a chalker, as it will brush away as you work.

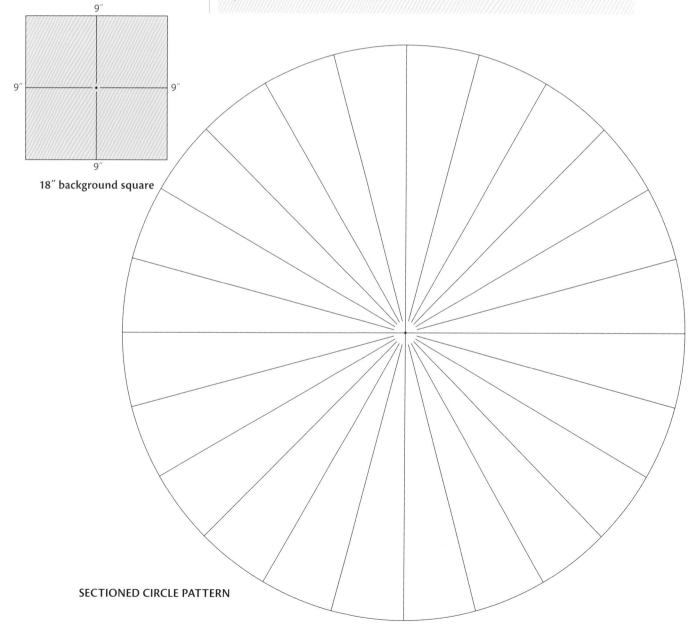

18″ background square

SECTIONED CIRCLE PATTERN

5. Position the edge of a long ruler or straightedge so it aligns with a radial line on the paper and the center dot. Extend the 2 corresponding radial lines from the paper to the fabric. Repeat for all lines. Remember to adjust the ruler edge to accommodate the marking tool you are using. This process must be done accurately, because the lines you draw are guidelines for positioning the squares. Make them as thin as you can and still be able to see them. The lines should go to the edge of your fabric square, as they will help guide you when it is time to trim the 18″ square.

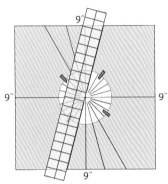

**Paper circle on fabric background,
with lines extended outward**

6. Once all lines are marked outside the paper circle, remove the circle and extend the lines inward toward the center dot, stopping just before the dot.

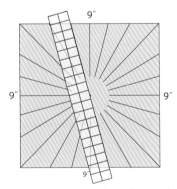

**Remove paper circle and extend
lines inward.**

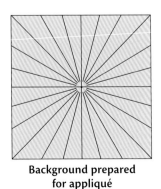

**Background prepared
for appliqué**

APPLIQUÉ PREPARATION

The following freezer-paper method produces crisp, sharp corners and well-shaped squares. You will need 12 fabric squares of each size square (A–F). Each freezer-paper square can be used 6 times.

1. Smoothly press 2 squares 6″ × 6″ of freezer paper together, shiny side to dull side, making sure there are no wrinkles.

2. Trace 2 of each square (A–F) onto the dull side of the freezer paper. Mark the appropriate letter on each and cut out (or rotary cut the freezer paper based on the size stated inside each square).

3. Starting with the 2 A's, press the freezer paper A squares, shiny side down, onto the wrong side of the chosen fabric. I position the squares onto the fabric with the grain to give me a more stable square shape while still allowing some give. Cut around each paper square, allowing a ³/₁₆″ seam allowance.

4. Spray some starch into a small dish. Dip a small stencil brush or cotton swab into the starch and wet the seam allowance with the starch.

5. Using a toothpick or similar tool, bring the wet seam allowance over the freezer paper edge, a little at a time, while using a small hot iron to press and dry the fabric seam allowance in place.

6. When all seam allowances have been pressed over the paper edge, set aside to cool while you prepare the second A square.

7. While the second square is cooling, press the first one again. This warms the paper enough so you can easily

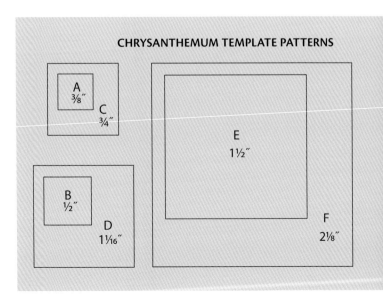

CHRYSANTHEMUM TEMPLATE PATTERNS

A
³/₈″

C
¾″

E
1½″

B
½″

D
1¹/₁₆″

F
2⅛″

DRAFTING FOR THE CREATIVE QUILTER

remove it by lifting a section of the seam allowance and removing the paper shape. (I use tweezers for this step.) Then repress the fabric shape and put it under a weight or book to let it cool. Use the just-removed paper square again and repeat Steps 3–6 to create another A square. While this new square is cooling, remove the paper from the other A square. You should constantly be working back and forth (6 from each paper square) to create 12 fabric squares from the 2 freezer paper A squares.

♦♦♦ Noteworthy ♦♦♦

I use two freezer-paper squares because it allows me to constantly be working with one or the other to create the 12 fabric squares I need without wasting time. If I cut 12 paper squares, the chance for discrepancy in size is increased.

8. Prepare the remaining squares (B–F) similarly to create 12 fabric squares of each size.

FABRIC SQUARES PLACEMENT

1. Holding an A square with tweezers, apply a tiny thin line of fabric glue in the middle of opposite seam allowances.

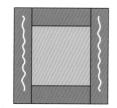

Glue along seam allowance.

2. Still holding the square by a corner with tweezers, place the square onto the background by moving it toward the center until each corner of the square lines up with a line on the background. Repeat for the remaining 11 A squares. Evaluate each square carefully, making any position adjustments or changes before moving to the next square. You are looking for sameness of fit all the way around. Appliqué all A's and then all B's for the best results.

3. Using matching-colored thread, appliqué each square in place. Be sure the squares are held securely and not shifting.

4. Position the 12 B squares between 2 A squares, matching their corners to marked lines on the background. Glue baste in place, evaluate, and appliqué. Repeat for C, D, E, and F fabric squares, each positioned between the 2 squares preceding it and aligning each corner to a line. *Do not press yet.* When all 72 squares are appliquéd, continue to use the marked lines on the background for the next steps.

5. Trim the appliqué block to an exact 16½″ square, using the horizontal, vertical, and diagonal lines on the background fabric for guidance. Chalk the cutting lines equidistant (8¼″) from the center horizontally and vertically and measure twice before cutting.

Position 12 A squares and appliqué in place.

6. The 3 different sizes of circle shapes (J, K, L) are prepared in the same way as the squares. You will need 18 dark blue J's, 7 dark blue K's, and 12 magenta L's. Refer to the photo (page 99) for placement.

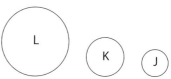

Template patterns J, K, and L

ADDING THE CIRCULAR ELEMENT

1. Take an 18″ square of plain or graph paper and fold it in half and then in half again. Do this carefully and make really sharp creases.

2. Using a compass, draw a quarter circle with a radius of 7¾″ on your folded paper. The center folds are your pivot point. Refer to page 19: How to Use a Compass to Draw a Circle. Holding the paper securely so it does not shift (you could staple it if you care to), cut the curve. You will be cutting 4 layers of paper; be accurate.

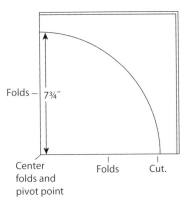

Folds — 7¾″

Center folds and pivot point   Folds   Cut.

Fold the paper and draw a quarter circle on it.

3. Open the paper. Place the paper circle onto the right side of the appliquéd block, matching the centers and creases with the center and lines on the background with pins, as you did previously. Tape this in place. Use a removable marker to draw a circle on the background, following the edge of the paper circle. (You are marking a 15½″ circle, 7¾″ radius, onto the background.)

4. Make a template (page 90) from shape I (pattern on page 115). Cut 4 I shapes from appropriate fabric and join to create a 16½″ square with a cut-out circle. (I waited until I was working on the design wall to do this, because in my quilt the 4 I's are

different fabrics that blend with the quilt background.)

5. Place the I square right side up on the 16½″ square appliquéd background. The 4 seams of the I shape should align with the horizontal and vertical lines on the background fabric. With right sides together, match and pin the raw edge of the 4 seams to the horizontal and vertical lines on the background where they intersect with the circle line. Working with a corner at a time, bring a corner to the center. With right sides together, continue to match and pin the raw edge of the I square to the circle line between the pins all the way around the circle. The appliqué block remains flat on the bottom while the I shape is pinned to the circle line on the block.

Position I over the block. Turn over and pin as the arrows indicate.

6. Sew the I shape to the background square with a ¼″ seam allowance; make sure this is smooth with no pleats. Evaluate your sewing carefully. Press the seam away from the circle. I do not trim the excess block fabric until I am ready to actually sew it into my quilt, then I trim the excess to the raw edges of the I shape.

PEACE SIGN

Appliqué, stencil, or paint the peace sign onto a 5″ × 6½″ (unfinished) piece of fabric.

Quilt Assembly

Now that the blocks are complete, you are ready to go to the design wall. Section it off and begin your process of folding and pinning fabric around the blocks. Sketch #3 (page 77) is your cutting and sewing guide. Measurements include the seam allowance, and the grid dimension is 1½″. Refer to Designing on an Overall Grid (page 71) to complete the sampler.

As a final touch, after the quilt is assembled, appliqué ¾″ × ¾″ squares to the borders in various places. Refer to pages 112–113 for appliqué instructions and to the photo on page 99 for placement ideas.

DRAFTING FOR THE CREATIVE QUILTER

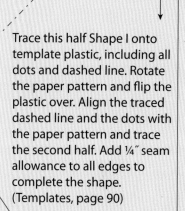

Trace this half Shape I onto template plastic, including all dots and dashed line. Rotate the paper pattern and flip the plastic over. Align the traced dashed line and the dots with the paper pattern and trace the second half. Add ¼″ seam allowance to all edges to complete the shape. (Templates, page 90)

Half of pattern I
Chrysanthemum

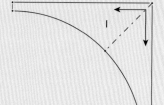

The complete template pattern I will have this shape. Add ¼″ seam allowance to all edges.

Sedona, 45½" × 45½", designed, pieced, and hand quilted by the author.

Sedona

Sedona was designed by fracturing one-eighth of the basic structure of a Carpenter's Wheel block and using mirrors to see the whole design. Once I have a design I like, I translate that to pattern shapes and make templates. Using the templates, I cut fabric shapes to create a rough-cut mock-up in actual size (page 91), which becomes my color map. Once I see my quilt in actual size, color, and fabric using mirrors, I cut fabric and sew the quilt. You may make *Sedona* in either size or make any changes you'd like. Refer to Designing within Traditional Blocks (page 79) to see how redesigning is done. Enjoy.

Fabric Requirements

Fabric requirements are approximate and will vary depending on your color map.

- **Gold:** 1 yard (2 yards) total for background

- **Deep darks:** ⅞ yard (1½ yards) total for star points

- **Medium lights:** ⅞ yard (1½ yards) total for star points

- **Accents:** ¾ yard (1¼ yards)

- **Two contrasting fabrics:** ⅓ yard (½ yard) each for sawtooth border

- **Print:** 1 yard (1⅔ yards) for Borders 2 and 4*

- **Accent:** ⅛ yard (⅛ yard) for Border 3

* Cut Border 4 on the lengthwise grain.

Vital Statistics

Drafting category: 8-pointed star

Number of pieces: 428 (524)

Number of shapes: 11 (13)

Color and Design

Begin by making very accurate templates (page 90). Then explore your color and fabric options and start cutting to make your "map," or rough-cut mock-up (page 91). Start in the center star area and develop Sedona Star outward. If you plan the center star and triangles and then the next layer of 16 star points, you can begin to sew. This much will have established all the color options. Remember, you don't need a lot of different colors, just a variety of value, intensity, and visual texture options. The outer layer of 24 star points will echo the colors in the center sections, but they could and will change in design and fabric slightly. The outer layer should support, enhance, and relate to the center area to create a oneness. Be open and willing to change and then always ask yourself if the changes you make are improving the color and design. Don't be in a hurry to sew until you have exhausted all your options and have created a beautiful block. You don't need to be right the first time; just the last time. When working with split points, use two highly contrasting fabrics to create dimension.

Workmanship

This block is not extremely difficult to sew. It does, however, require you to be awake, present, and accounted for. It is a slow, choppy sewing process in many areas, though not a lot of chain piecing. Be willing to take your time. You will deal with many bias edges, so take extreme care with your iron; I suggest a hot, dry iron. Use your templates to monitor your work—this is critical to the success of the block in either size. This block is just like a jigsaw puzzle—each piece must fit exactly to the next. Trim seams to a generous ⅛" in the smaller, pieced areas, and pay close attention to your piecing illustrations and pressing paths. Cut and sew the center star and surrounding triangles first, then create the second layer of 16 star point units, and then the outer layer of 24 star point units and surrounding triangle units. Finally, assemble the quilt top.

Split diagram showing differences between the 18″ (bottom half) and 36″ (top half) *Sedona*

Center Star and Surrounding Triangles

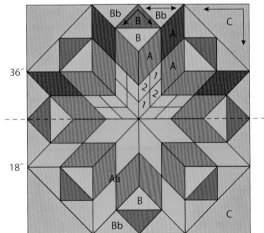

Center star and surrounding triangles

⟶	= pressing direction
⟷	= fabric grainline
⦶	= Y-seam
○	= seam pressed open

Cutting

Make accurate templates (page 90) for A, B, and C (pages 123–125), adding ¼″ seam allowances to all sides of each shape. Punch holes at the dots and transfer all reference lines, information, and grainline arrows. A and Aa are the same size and shape; only one template is required to reflect all reference lines and information. B and Bb are the same size and shape, but have two different grain-placement arrows; only 1 template is needed. Shape C (the large triangle shape that holds the 4 B's) will also be used later as Cc. Make only 1 C template reflecting grain placement arrows on the corner and the long leg.

A: Cut 8 from deep dark and 16 from medium light for the 36″ *Sedona* design only.

Aa: Cut 8 from the oversized unit.

B: Cut 8 from an accent and 8 from medium light, with the straight grain on the corner.

Bb: Cut 16 from background, with the straight grain on the long leg.

C: Cut 4 from background, with the straight grain on the corner.

A/AA DIAMOND UNITS

Aa unit

1. If you are making the 36″ *Sedona* design, you have already cut 24 A diamonds; set these aside.

For both the 18″ and the 36″ *Sedona*, cut 1 strip 1¼″ × 42″ from

each of 2 fabrics—an accent and a medium light.

2. Sew Strip 1 to 2, offsetting them by the finished width of the strip. Press the seam open and trim the seam allowance to a generous ⅛″. Keeping the strip unit right side up, cut one end of the strip unit at a 45° angle and cut 16 segments 1¼″ wide.

Cut and sew the strips, then cut the segments.

3. Pair 2 appropriate segments together turning one to align the colors, and make a mark over the seam ¼″ from the sewing edge on both segments. Pin the intersection and sew. Check to be sure the intersection is perfectly matched before pressing the seam open and trimming off the dog ears.

Pair, pin, and sew 2 segments together.

4. Place the A/Aa template face down on the wrong side of the fabric diamond. Align the center and lines of the template with the intersection and the seams of the oversized fabric unit. Mark the dots and carefully cut around the template with a very small rotary cutter. Make 8.

Custom cut Aa from the oversized unit; make 8.

5. If you are making the 18″ Sedona Star, skip this step and proceed to the B/Bb triangle unit. If you are making the 36″ Sedona Star, join 3 A's to 1 Aa; make 8. Set aside.

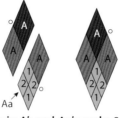

Join A's and Aa's; make 8.

B/BB TRIANGLE UNITS
Arrange 2 B's and 2 Bb's, paying attention to appropriate grain placement. Join 2 B's and press the seam open. Join a Bb to each side of the BB unit. Press toward the Bb's; Make 8.

BbBB unit; make 8.

A DIAMONDS AND B TRIANGLES
1. Arrange 2 A diamond units and a B triangle unit. The Y-seam area is circled. Stop sewing just before the dot and backstitch.

2. Join an A unit to the B unit, pinning at the dots and matching points. Sew from the edge to the dot and backstitch. Repeat for the second A unit. To be able to sew from the edge to the dot both times, the diamond will be on top once and the triangle will be on top once.

3. Now join the 2 diamonds, pinning at the dots and matching the

seams; sew from the center edge to the dot and backstitch. Press the triangle seams to the diamond, then press the diamond seam open. Trim the seam allowance to a generous ⅛″. Make 4.

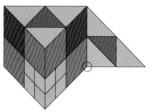

Join 2 A diamonds to a B triangle; make 4.

4. Join a B unit to the right side of each AAB unit. Pin at the dots and sew from the edge to the dot and backstitch.

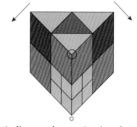

Join B to the right side of AAB; make 4.

5. Join 2 AABB units together to make 2 halves; make 2. First sew from the outside edge to the dot and backstitch. Next sew from the center edge to the dot and backstitch. Press the triangle seams to the diamond; then press the diamond seam open. Trim the seam allowance to a generous ⅛″.

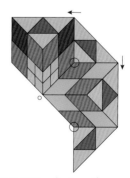

Sew 2 AABB units together; make 2.

6. Join the 2 halves. Sew the center seam last. Press the triangle seams

toward the diamonds; then press the diamond seams open.

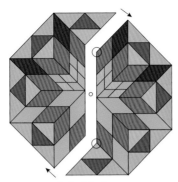

Join 2 halves.

7. Join a C triangle (straight grain on the 2 short sides) to the 4 corners and press toward C. The center star and triangles are complete.

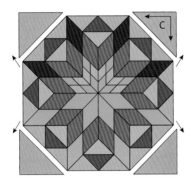

Join 4 C's to the corners.

Second Layer of Star Points

CUTTING

You have already made the C template but will now use it as Cc and place the straight of grain on the long leg of the triangle. Make templates (page 90) for D, E, and F (pages 123–125), adding ¼″ seam allowances to all sides of each shape. Punch holes at the dots and transfer all the reference lines, information, and grainline arrows.

Cc: Cut 4 from background, with grainline on the long leg of the triangle.

D: Cut 8 from strip unit.

E: Cut 8 from strip unit.

F: Cut 8 from background.

Fr: Cut 8 from background (turn over template F).

D UNITS

1. Cut 1 strip 2″ × 40″ (2 strips 3″ × 40″) from each of 2 fabrics—a deep dark and a medium light.

2. Sew together a strip from each fabric, press the seam open, and trim the seam allowance to a generous ⅛″.

3. Place the D template face down on the wrong side of the strip unit, make dots, and cut 8. Set aside.

Caution: Be aware of how you are placing this template onto the fabric strip unit. Note which half of the shape (left or right) will be dark and be consistent. It is very easy to make an error here.

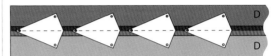

Cut 8 D's from the strip unit.

E UNITS

1. Cut 1 strip 1½″ × 40″ (2 strips 2¼″ × 40″) from each of 2 fabrics—a deep dark and a medium light.

2. Sew together a strip from each fabric, press the seam open, and trim the seam allowance to a generous ⅛″.

3. Place the E template face down on the wrong side of the strip unit, mark the dots, and cut 8. (See Caution.)

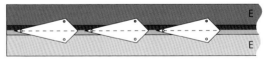

Cut 8 E's from the strip unit.

EF/FR UNITS

Join an F and Fr to each side of 8 E units. Press the seams away from E.

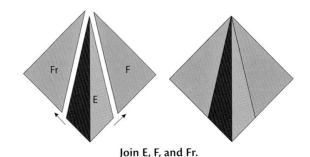

Join E, F, and Fr.

DRAFTING FOR THE CREATIVE QUILTER

CCDEF/FR UNIT

Assemble 4 CcDEF/Fr units; 4 EF/Fr units will remain. Set all aside.

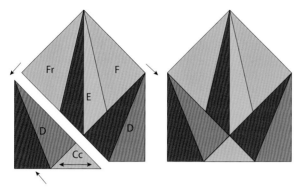

Assemble CcDEF/Fr units; make 4.

Outer Layer of Star Points

CUTTING

Make templates for G, H, and I, adding ¼" seam allowances to all sides of each shape. Punch holes at the dots and transfer all reference lines, information, and grainline arrows. Shapes G and Gg are the same size and shape; only one template is required to reflect all lines.

G: Cut 24 from accent and 48 from medium light for 36" *Sedona* design only.

Gg: Cut 24 from oversized unit.

H: Cut 24 from deep dark and 24 from medium light.

I: Cut 24 from a strip unit.

G/GG UNITS

The process for making the G unit and the Gg unit is the same as for A and Aa (page 118).

1. If you are making the 36" *Sedona*, you have already cut 72 A diamond shapes; set them aside.

2. For both the 18" and 36" *Sedona*, cut 2 strips 1¼" × 40" from each of 2 fabrics.

3. Sew Strip 1 to 2, offsetting by the finished width of the strip. Press the seams open and trim the seam allowance to a generous ⅛". Keeping strip units right side up, cut one end at a 45° angle. Cut 24 segments 1" (1¼") from each strip unit.

4. Pair 2 appropriate segments together and make a mark over the seam ¼" from the sewing edge on both segments. Pin the intersection and sew. When the intersection is perfectly matched, press the seam open and trim. Make 24.

5. Place the Gg template face down on the wrong side of the oversized fabric diamond (see page 119). Align the center and the lines of the template with the intersection and seams of the fabric. Mark the dots and carefully cut around the template. Make 24.

6. If you are making the 36" *Sedona*, join 3 G's to a Gg; make 24.

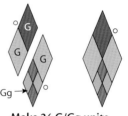

Make 24 G/Gg units.

I UNITS

1. Cut 2 strips 2" × 40" (4 strips 3" × 40") from each of 2 fabrics—a deep dark and a medium light.

2. Sew together a strip from each fabric. Press the seam open and trim the seam allowance to a generous ⅛".

3. Place the I template face down on the wrong side of the strip unit. Mark the dots and carefully cut around the template. Cut 24. (See Caution, page 120.)

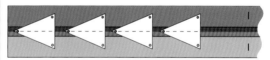

Cut 24 I's.

G/GG, H, AND I UNITS

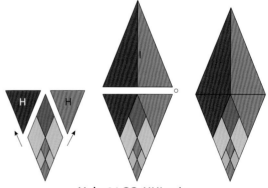

Make 24 GGgHHI units.

Outer Layer of Triangles

CUTTING

Make templates for J and K, adding ¼″ seam allowances to all sides of each shape. Punch holes at the dots and transfer all reference lines, information, and grainline arrows.

J: Cut 64: 16 from an accent, 16 from medium light, and 32 from background.

K: Cut 48: 16 from an accent and 32 from background.

JK UNITS

1. Arrange 4 J's. Join 2 J's together, press the seam open, and trim the seam allowance to a generous ⅛″.

2. Add the remaining 2 J's to each side of the JJ unit; make 16.

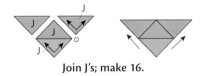

Join J's; make 16.

3. Join 3 K's together; press and trim. Make 16.

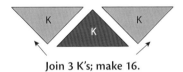

Join 3 K's; make 16.

4. Join the J unit and the K unit; press open and trim. Make 16.

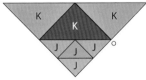

Join J's to K's; make 16.

LARGE CORNER L TRIANGLES

Cut 2 squares 7″ × 7″ (12″ × 12″) from the background fabric. Cut in half diagonally and set aside.

Sedona Assembly

1. Add 2 GHI diamond units to a CcDEF unit; press and trim. Make 4.

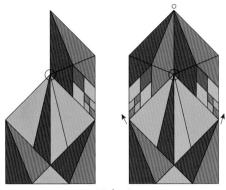

Make 4.

2. Add 2 GHI diamond units to a JK unit; press and trim. Make 8.

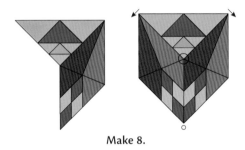

Make 8.

3. Add 2 GHIJK units to an EF unit; press and trim. Make 4.

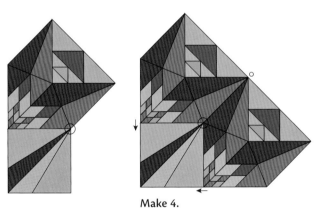

Make 4.

DRAFTING FOR THE CREATIVE QUILTER

4. Add a JK unit to each side of an EFGHIJK unit; press and trim. Make 4.

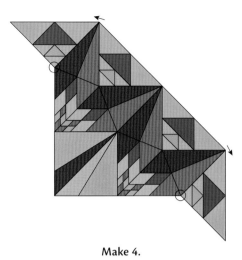

Make 4.

5. Arrange all units and the center star. Assemble as shown.

6. Add the oversized L triangles to each corner, pressing toward the L triangles. Trim the triangles to the edge of the Sedona Star. The Sedona Star should now measure 18½″ (36½″) unfinished.

Sedona Star assembly

SEDONA TEMPLATE PATTERNS; ADD ¼″ SEAM ALLOWANCES TO ALL SIDES OF ALL LETTERED SHAPES.

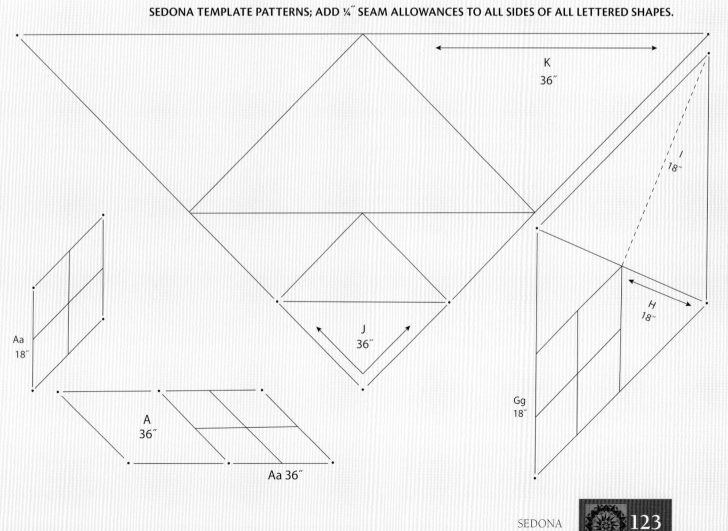

K
36″

I
18″

H
18″

Aa
18″

J
36″

Gg
18″

A
36″

Aa 36″

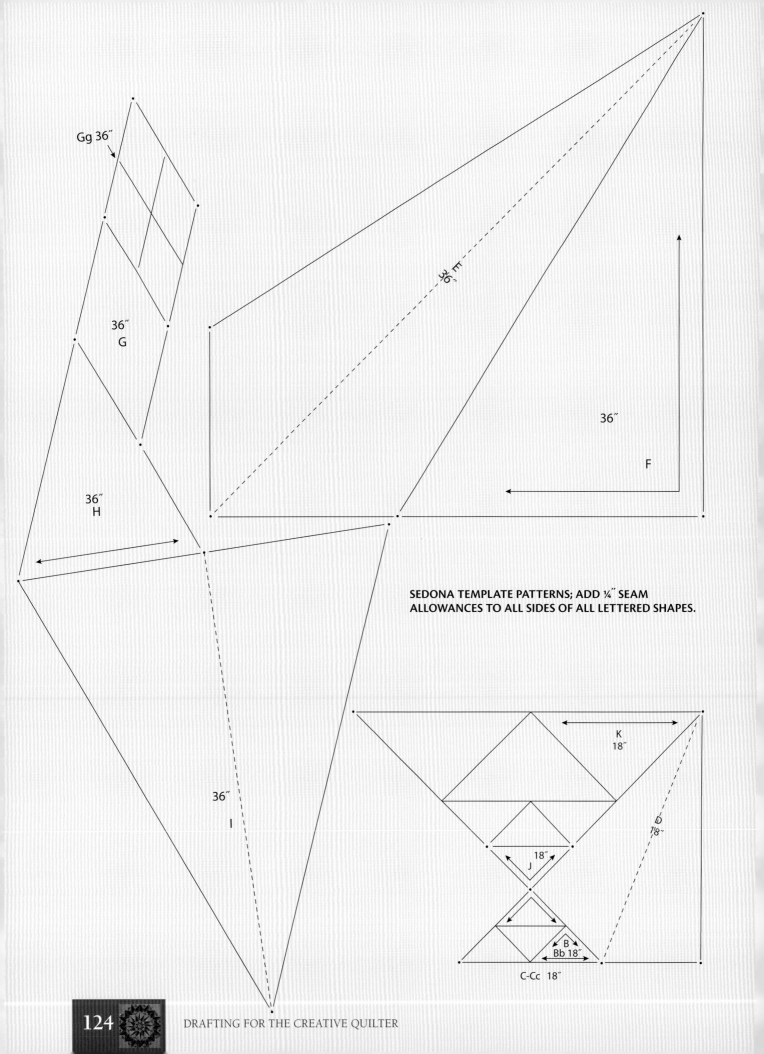

Gg 36"

36"
G

36"
H

36"
FF

36"

F

SEDONA TEMPLATE PATTERNS; ADD ¼" SEAM
ALLOWANCES TO ALL SIDES OF ALL LETTERED SHAPES.

36"

I

K
18"

D
18"

J 18"

B
Bb 18"

C-Cc 18"

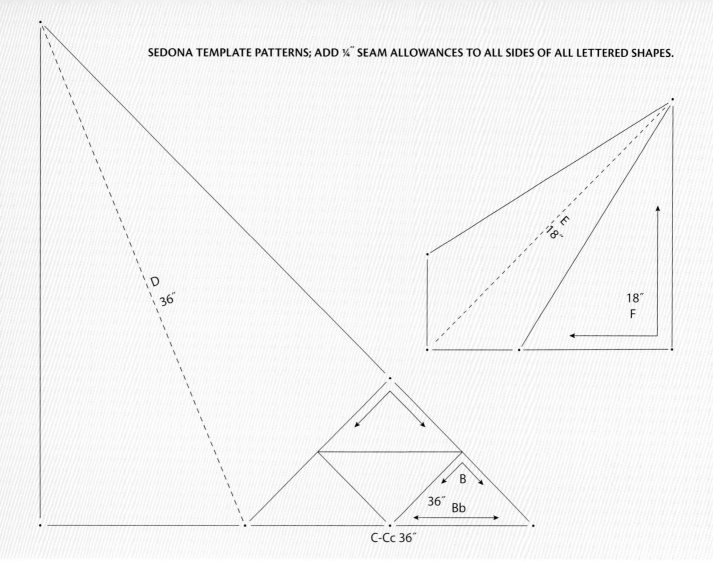

SEDONA TEMPLATE PATTERNS; ADD ¼" SEAM ALLOWANCES TO ALL SIDES OF ALL LETTERED SHAPES.

D 36"

E 18"

18" F

B

36" Bb

C-Cc 36"

Borders

Four borders are added to *Sedona*—one pieced border and three plain fabric borders—in varying finished widths of ⅜", ¼", and 2⅝" (3⅝"). These borders are added to the quilt in a boxed-corner fashion, meaning you add two sides and then the top and bottom. The quilt measures 18" (36") square finished, 18½" (36½") square unfinished.

Measure your own quilt. If your measurements are different from mine, measure and cut lengths based on your quilt from this point forward.

BORDER 1: SAWTOOTH BORDER

You need a total of 148 (292) sawteeth—36 (72) per side plus 4 corner sawteeth.

1. Cut 74 (146) squares 2" × 2" from 2 different fabrics.

2. Pair 1 square of each fabric 74 (146) times.

3. Draw a line diagonally on the lightest square in each pair.

4. Sew ¼" from the line on both sides.

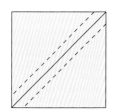

Sew ¼" on both sides of the drawn line.

5. Cut on the drawn line.

Cut on the drawn line.

6. Press the seam open and trim the seam allowance to a generous ⅛".

7. Custom cut a 1" square from each.

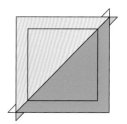

Make 148 (292) 1" sawteeth.

8. Join 18 (36) sawteeth together 4 times in one diagonal direction and 4 times in the opposite direction.

Make 4 of each.

9. Join a sawtooth unit from each diagonal direction; make 4.

Make 4.

10. Add a sawtooth to each end of 2 sawtooth units. Note the orientation of the diagonal.

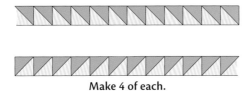

Make 2.

11. Add the sawtooth units from Step 9 to 2 sides of the quilt and press toward the quilt.

12. Add the 2 sawtooth units from Step 10 with corner sawteeth to the top and bottom of the quilt and press toward the quilt. The quilt now measures 19″ (37″) finished, 19½ (37½″) unfinished.

Add borders to the quilt.
Noteworthy: The amount of sawteeth in the first border will be double for the 36″ version of *Sedona*, see photo page 116.

BORDER 2: ³/₈″ FINISHED

1. Cut 2 strips ⅞″ × 19½″ (⅞″ × 37½″) and add to the sides of the quilt top.

2. Cut 2 strips ⅞″ × 20¼″ (⅞″ × 38¼″) and add to the top and bottom.

BORDER 3: ¹/₄″ FINISHED

1. Cut 2 strips ¾″ × 20¼″ (¾″ × 38¼″) and add to the sides of the quilt top.

2. Cut 2 strips ¾″ × 20¾″ (¾″ × 38¾″) and add to the top and bottom.

BORDER 4: 2⁵/₈″ FINISHED FOR 18″ *SEDONA*

1. Cut 2 strips 3⅛″ × 20¾″ and add to the sides of the quilt top.

2. Cut 2 strips 3⅛″ × 26″ and add to the top and bottom.

BORDER 4: 3⁵/₈″ FINISHED FOR 36″ *SEDONA*

1. Cut 2 strips 4⅛″ × 38¾″ and add to the sides of the quilt top.

2. Cut 2 strips 4⅛″ × 46″ and add to the top and bottom.

BIBLIOGRAPHY

Beyer, Jinny, *Patchwork Patterns*, McLean, VA: EPM Publications, 1979.

Brackman, Barbara, *Encyclopedia of Pieced Quilt Patterns*, Paducah, KY: American Quilter's Society, 1993.

Garber, Gail, *Stellar Journeys*, Paducah, KY: American Quilter's Society, 2001.

Hall, Jane, and Dixie Haywood, *Perfect Pineapples*, Lafayette, CA: C&T Publishing, 1989.

Martin, Judy, *Shining Star Quilts*, Montrose, PA; Moon over the Mountain Publishing, 1987.

McCloskey, Marsha, *Feathered Star Quilts*, Woodinville, WA: That Patchwork Place, 1988.

McClun, Diana, and Laura Nownes, *Quilts Galore!*, New York, NY: McGraw-Hill, 1991.

Pasquini, Katie, *Mandala*, Lafayette, CA: C&T Publishing, 1983.

Pippin, Kitty, *Quilting with Japanese Fabrics*, Woodinville, WA: That Patchwork Place, 2000.

Quilter's Newsletter Magazine, Drafting Articles, October 1994 to November 1995.

Reis, Sherry, *Basic Quiltmaking Techniques for Eight-Pointed Stars*, Woodinville, WA: That Patchwork Place, 1999.

Squier-Craig, Sharon, *Drafting Plus*, Montrose, PA: Chitra Publications, 1994.

Venters, Diana, and Elaine Krajenke Ellison, *Mathematical Quilts*, Emeryville, CA: Key Curriculum Press, 1999.

Wolfrom, Joen, *The Visual Dance*, Lafayette, CA: C&T Publishing, 1995.

ABOUT THE AUTHOR

Sally Collins is an award-winning quiltmaker, teacher, and author of a DVD titled *Sally Collins Teaches You Precision Piecing* and of four previously published books, *Small Scale Quiltmaking*; *The Art of Machine Piecing*; *Borders, Bindings, and Edges*; and *Mastering Precision Piecing*.

She took her first quiltmaking class in 1978 and quickly discovered the pleasure and joy of making quilts. Although she is most recognized for her quality workmanship and teaching expertise, her continual interest is in the process of quiltmaking—the journey. She loves the challenge of combining design, color, and intricate piecing in a traditional style. Through this book, Sally hopes to open the door to creative freedom as she guides, encourages, and challenges quilters to draft and design their own work, from start to finish.

Sally spends her time traveling across the country, conducting workshops, giving presentations, and enjoying life with her husband, Joe; son, Sean; and grandchildren, Kaylin, Joey, and Lucas. Sally can be reached at www.sallycollins.org.

Also by Sally Collins

Great Titles *from* C&T PUBLISHING

Available at your local retailer or **www.ctpub.com** *or* **800-284-1114**

For a list of other fine books from C&T Publishing, ask for a free catalog:

C&T PUBLISHING, INC.
P.O. Box 1456
Lafayette, CA 94549
800-284-1114

Email: ctinfo@ctpub.com
Website: www.ctpub.com

C&T Publishing's professional photography services are now available to the public. Visit us at www.ctmediaservices.com.

Tips and Techniques can be found at www.ctpub.com > Consumer Resources > Quiltmaking Basics: Tips & Techniques for Quiltmaking & More

For quilting supplies:

COTTON PATCH
1025 Brown Ave.
Lafayette, CA 94549
Store: 925-284-1177
Mail order: 925-283-7883

Email: CottonPa@aol.com
Website: www.quiltusa.com

Note: Fabrics used in the quilts shown may not be currently available, as fabric manufacturers keep most fabrics in print for only a short time.